COLLINS

HANDY TOWN PLAN ATLAS
BRITAIN

CONTENTS

Published by Collins
An imprint of HarperCollins*Publishers*
77-85 Fulham Palace Road, Hammersmith, London W6 8JB

The HarperCollins website address is: www.**fire**and**water**.com

Copyright © HarperCollins*Publishers* Ltd 2000
Mapping © Bartholomew Ltd 1997, 1999, 2000

Collins® is a registered trademark of HarperCollins*Publishers* Limited

Mapping generated from Bartholomew digital databases

Bartholomew website address is:

Town and city centre maps on pa
41, 57, 63, 75, 81, 83, 87, 91, 99, 10
Survey Mapping with the permi

r footpath is no evidence of a right of

976 4   MC10234   LNN

991910479   5

HarperCollins*Publishers*

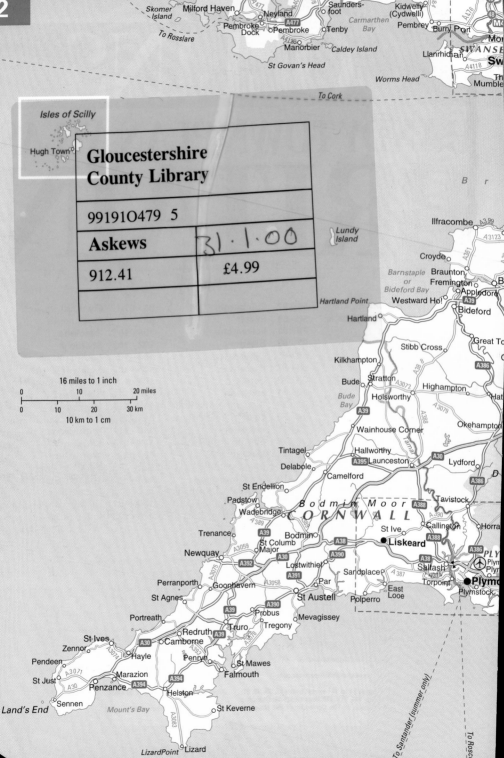

16 miles to 1 inch

0 — 10 — 20 miles

0 — 10 — 20 — 30 km

10 km to 1 cm

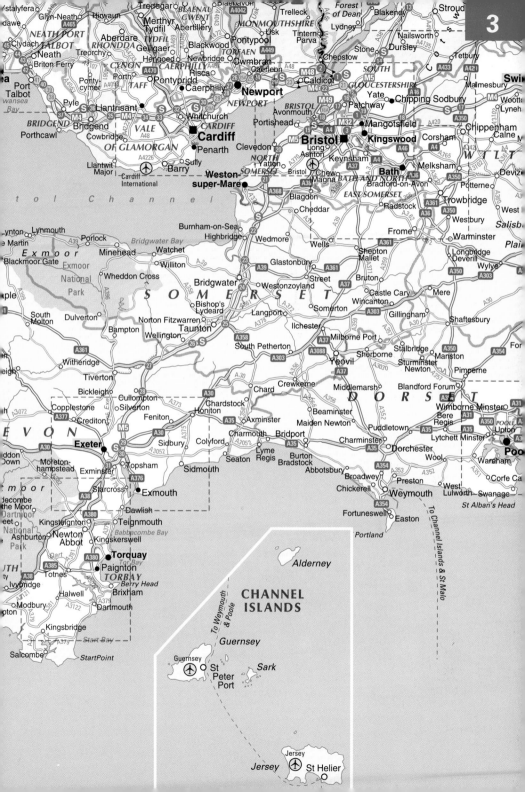

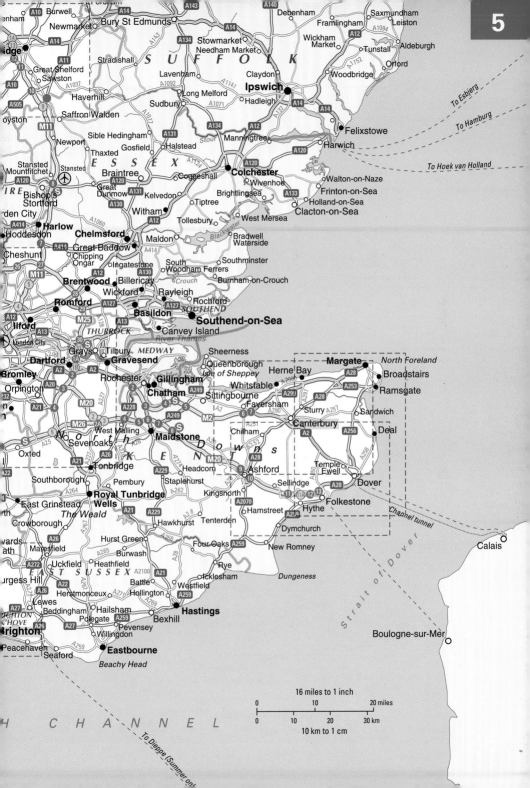

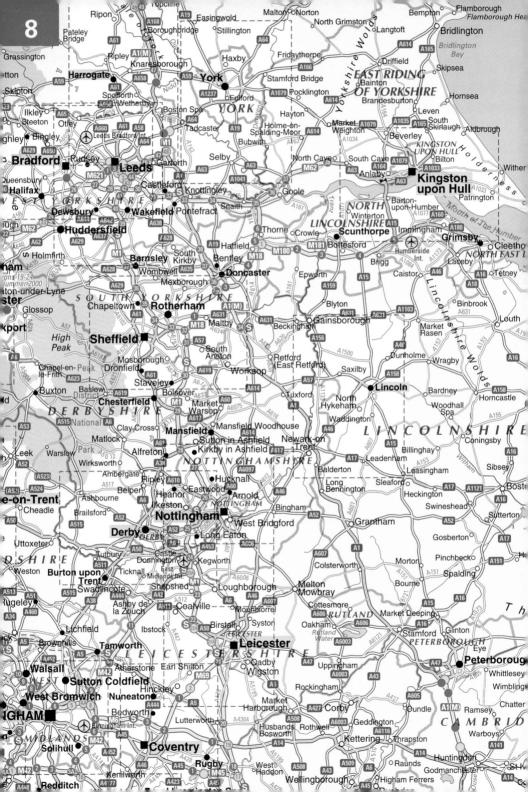

16 miles to 1 inch

0   10   20 miles

0   10   20   30 km

10 km to 1 cm

gton

rn Head

OLNSHIRE

To Rotterdam & Zeebrugge

th

nercotes

Mablethorpe

Maltby le Marsh

Alford

Ingoldmells

ney

sby   Burgh   Skegness
le Marsh

Wainfleet
All Saints

/rangle

Blakeney
Point

Brancaster   Blakeney   Sheringham

The   Hunstanton   Wells-next-
the-Sea   Holt   Cromer

Wash   Heacham   Mundesley

Snettisham   Docking   North   Happisburgh
Walsham

ch   Dersingham   Fakenham

Stalham

King's   South Wootton   Guist   Cawston   Coltishall   Hemsby
Lynn   Bawdeswell

utton   NORFOLK   Hoveton   The   Caister-on-Sea
ridge

A1101   Narborough   East   Norwich   Acle   Great
Dereham   Sprowston   Yarmouth

Wisbech   Necton   Broads

Outwell   Swaffham   Norwich   Hopton
Corton

Stradsett   Wymondham   Brooke   Loddon
March   Downham   Watton   Haddiscoe   Oulton
Market   Beccles   Lowestoft

Southery   Attleborough   Long
Methwold   Mundford   Stratton   Bungay   Kessingland

Larling   Homersfield   Brampton
Thetford Forest   Harleston

Littleport   Brandon   Diss   Halesworth   Southwold
ESHIRE   Lakenheath   Park   Thetford   Scole

on   Ely   Mildenhall   Eye   Westleton

Stretham   Icklingham   Stanton   Saxmundham
rith   Ixworth   Leiston

Burwell   Fordham   Debenham   Framlingham

Newmarket   Bury St Edmunds

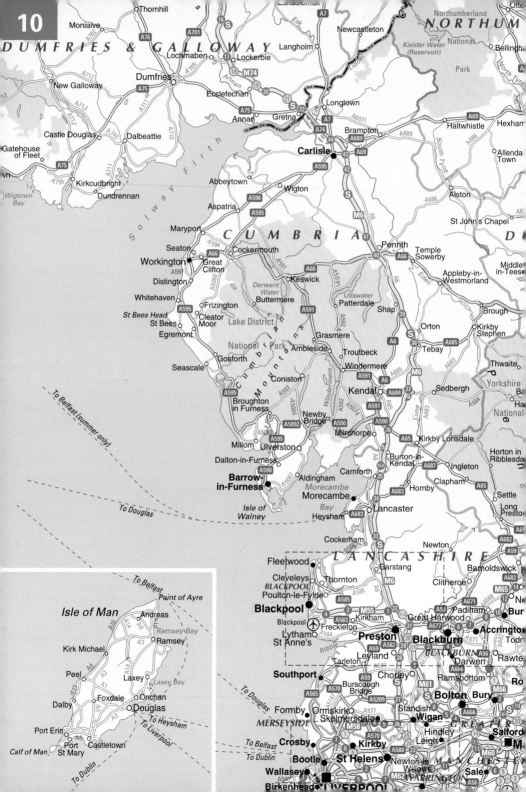

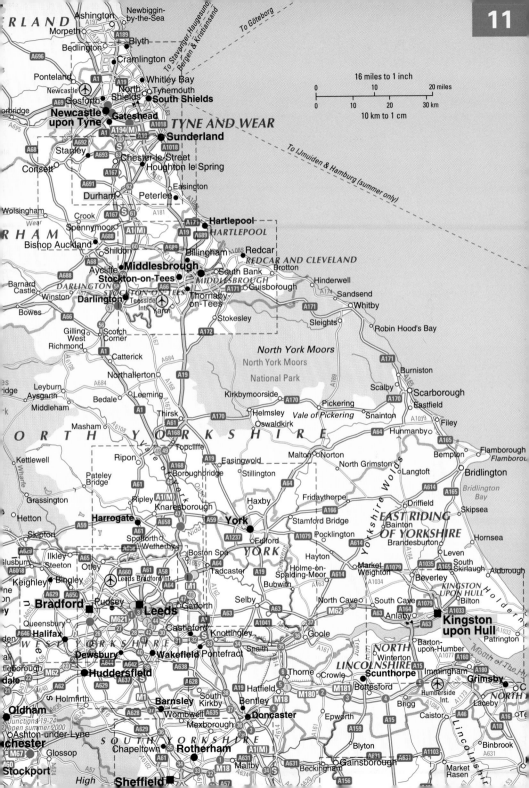

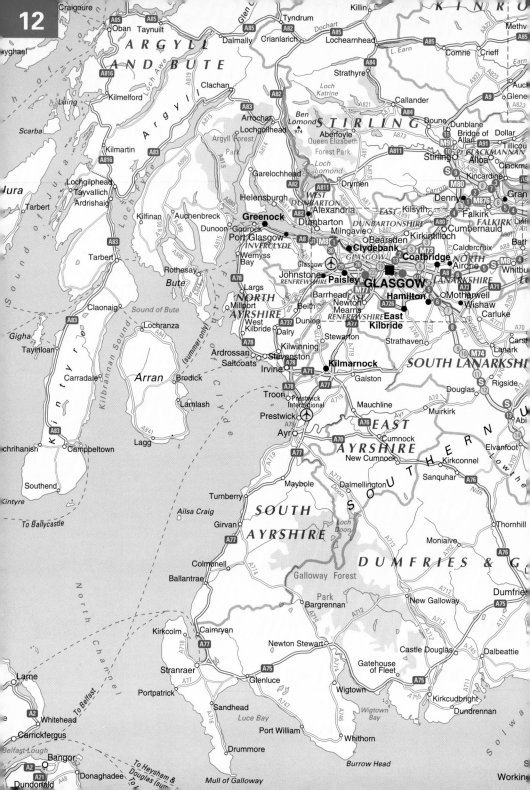

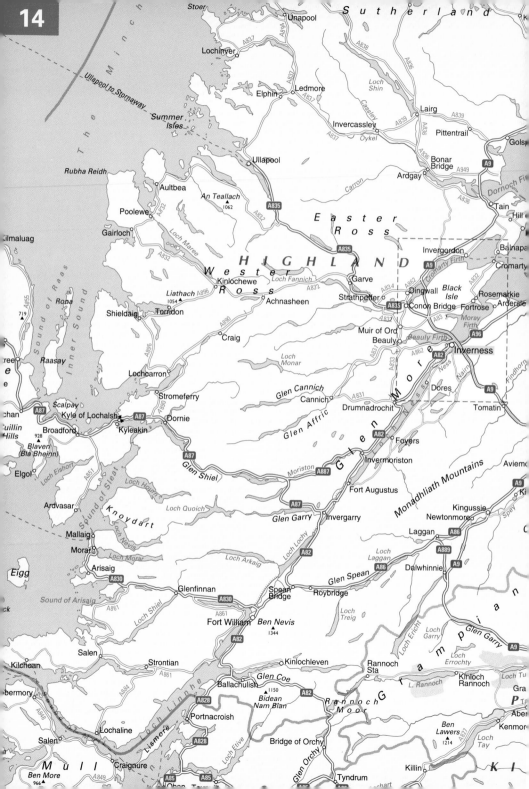

S U T H E R L A N D

The Minch

Ullapool to Stornaway

Summer Isles

Stoer
Unapool
Lochinver
Ledmore
Elphin
A837
A838
A894
A837
Loch Shin
A839
Lairg
Pittentrail
Invercassley
Oykel
Cassley
A836
Golsp
Bonar Bridge
A949
Ardgay
A836
Dornoch Fi
Tain
Hill

Rubha Reidh
Aultbea
Poolewe
Gairloch
An Teallach
▲1062
A835
E a s t e r
R o s s
A835
Invergordon
Balnapa
Cromarty
Cromarty Firth
A862
Rosemarkie
Ardersie
Fortrose

Kilmaluag
Loch Maree
A832
H I G H L A N D
W e s t e r
R o s s
Garve
A835
A834
Dingwall
Black Isle
Moray Firth
A96

Roña
Sound of Raasay
719 ▲
Liathach
▲1054
A896
Kinlochewe
Loch Fannich
A832
Strathpeffer
A835
Conon Bridge
A835
A832
Muir of Ord
Beauly
Beauly Firth
A862
Inverness
A9

Raasay
Inner Sound
Shieldaig
Torridon
Achnasheen
A890
Craig
A896
Loch Monar
A831
Cannich
Glen Cannich
Drumnadrochit
A82
Dores
A9
Tomatin

ree
Scalpay
A87
Kyle of Lochalsh
A87
Dornie
Stromeferry
A890
Lochcarron
Glen Affric
A831
Foyers
A82
Ness

chan
uillin Hills
Broadford
Kyleakin
A87
Glen Shiel
Moriston
A887
Invermoriston
Monadhliath Mountains
Aviem

Blaven
(Bla Bheinn)
928 ▲
Elgol
Loch Eishort
A851
Loch Hourn
Glen Shiel
A87
Fort Augustus
A9
Kingussie
Newtonmore

Ardvasar
Sound of Sleat
K n o y d a r t
Loch Quoich
Glen Garry
A87
Invergarry
A82
Laggan
A86
Ki

Mallaig
Morar
Loch Nevis
Loch Morar
Loch Arkaig
Loch Lochy
Loch Laggan
A889
Dalwhinnie
A86

Eigg
Arisaig
A830
Sound of Arisaig
A861
Glenfinnan
A830
Loch Shiel
A861
Spean Bridge
Roybridge
Glen Spean
A86
Loch Treig
Loch Ericht
Glen Garry
A9

ck
Salen
Kilchoan
Strontian
A861
A830
A861
Fort William
Ben Nevis
▲1344
Kinlochleven
Rannoch Sta
Loch Garry
Loch Errochty
Kinloch Rannoch
Loch Tu
Gra

bermory
Salen
Lochaline
Portnacroish
Ballachulish
Glen Coe
Bidean Nam Bian
1150 ▲
A828
A82
Rannoch Moor
L. Rannoch
Aber
Kenmor

Mull
Ben More
966 ▲
Craignure
A849
A85
A85
Bridge of Orchy
Glen Orchy
Ben Lawers
▲1214
Loch Tay
Killin
KI

A82
A384
A828
Loch Linnhe
Lismore
Loch Etive
Tyndrum
Kenmor

Grampian

Dornoch
Ross
A862
A833
A82
Glen More
Findhorn
A9

Loch Ness
A82

Eigg

Oban to Lochboisdale

Oban to Castlebay

Muck

Morar
Arisaig
Loch Morar
Loch Arkaig
A830
Glenfinnan
A830
A861
Spean Bridge
A82
Ro

Sound of Arisaig
A861
Fort William
Ben Nevis
1344

Salen
Strontian
A861
Kinlochleven

Coll

Kilchoan
Tobermory
A884
Ballachulish
Glen Coe
1150
Bidean
Nam Bian
A82

Tiree

Salen
Lochaline
A848
Portnacroish
A828
Bridge of Orchy

Mull
Craignure
A849
Lismore
Loch Etive
A828

Ben More
966

Oban
Taynuilt
A85
A85
Dalmally
A85

Iona
Fionnphort
A849
Pennyghael

ARGYLL
AND BUTE

Clachan

Luing
Kilmelford
Loch Awe
A819
Arrochar
A83
Lochgoil

Scarba
Argyll Forest Park
Gare

Colonsay
Scalasaig

Kilmartin
A83
A816
Argyll
Helensb

Oronsay

Jura
Tarbert
Lochgilphead
Tayvallich
Ardrishaig
A816

Kilfinan
Auchenbreck
Green

Dunoon
Gourock
Port Glas
INVER

Port Askaig
A846
A83
Tarbert
Loch Fyne
A886
Wemyss Bay

Islay
A847
A846
Bowmore
Loch Indaal
Rothesay
Bute
A815
Largs
Millport
NORTH
West Kilbride
AYRSHI

Portnahaven
Claonaig
Sound of Bute
A78

Gigha
A83
Lochranza
A841
Ardrossan
Saltcoats
A78
Irv

Tayinloan
(summer only)
Brodick

Port Ellen
Mull Of Oa
Kintyre
Carradale
Arran
Lamlash
Tr
Pre

16 miles to 1 inch

0   10   20 miles
0 10 20 30 km

10 km to 1 cm

Machrihanish
A83
Campbeltown
Lagg
A841

Southend
Mull of Kintyre
Turnberry
SE

Rathlin Island
To Ballycastle
Ailsa Craig
Girvan
AY

Portrush
Portstewart
A2
Bushmills
Bush
A29
Ballycastle
A44
Armoy
Cushendun
A77

Coleraine
A26
Colmonell
A77

Rubha Robhanais

Port Nis

Barabhas

Tolsta Head

Carlabhagh

Loch a' Tuath

Port nan Giuran

Great Bernera

Stornoway (Steornabhagh)

Miavaig

Gearraidh na h-Aibhne

Lewis (Eilean Leodhais)

Loch Langavat

A859

Scarp

Kebock Head

North Harris

WESTERN ISLES (NA H-EILEANAN AN IAR)

An Tairbeart

Shiant Islands

Rubha Reidh

Scalpay (Eilean Scalpaigh)

Taobh Tuath

South Harris

Pabbay

Loch Tarber

Roghadal

Rubha Hunish

Kilmaluag

Poolewe

Gairloch

Sound of Harris

Baile Mhartainn

Uig

Rona

Shieldaig

North Uist (Uibhist a' Tuath)

Lochmaddy (Loch na Madadh)

Loch Snizort

A855

719

Sound of Raas

A890

Heisker or Monach Islands

Loch Dunvegan

A87

Borve

Inner Sound

Lochcar

Benbecula (Beinn na Faoghla)

A850

Dunvegan

Portree

Raasay

A896

Skye

Bracadale

South Uist (Uibhist a' Deas)

Loch Bracadale

A863

Sligachan

Scalpay

Kyle of Lochalsh

A87

Kyleakin

Little Minch

Cuillin Hills

928 Blaven (Bla Bheinn)

Broadford

Lochboisdale (Loch Baghasdail)

(summer only)

Soay

Elgol

Loch Eishort

Spund of Sleat

Loch Hour

Eriskay (Eiriosgaigh)

Canna

Ardvasar

Knoydart

Pabbay

Rum (Rhum)

Mallaig

Loch Nevis

Barra (Eilean Barraigh)

Vatersay (Bhatarsaigh)

Castlebay (Bagh a' Chaisteil)

Morar

Loch Morar

Arisaig

A830

Pabaigh

Eigg

Oban to Lochboisdale

Mingulay (Miughalaigh)

Muck

Sound of Arisaig

A861

Loch Sh

Oban to Castlebay

Salen

The Minch

Ullapool to Stornoway

Rubha Reidh

Little Minch

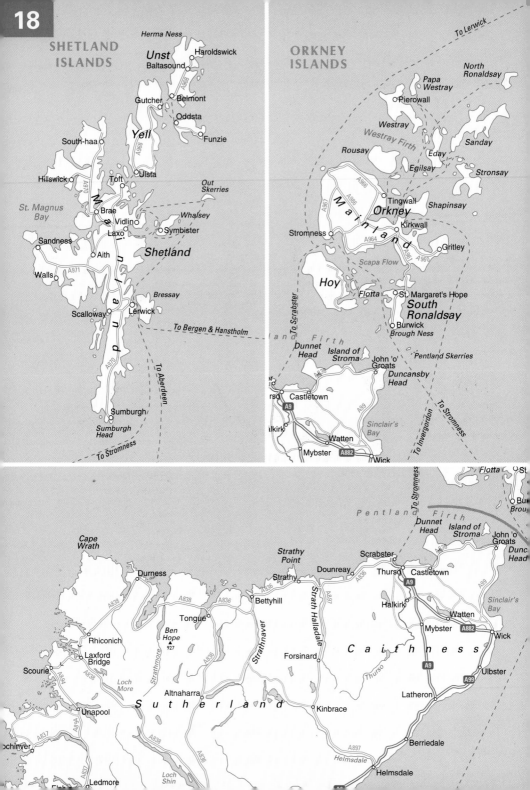

SHETLAND ISLANDS

Herma Ness
Unst
Haroldswick
Baltasound
Gutcher · Belmont
Oddsta
Yell
Funzie
South-haa
Ulsta
Hillswick · Toft
St. Magnus Bay
Brae
Vidlin
Laxo
Sandness
Symbister
Shetland
Whalsey
Out Skerries
Aith
Walls
Bressay
Scalloway
Lerwick
To Bergen & Hantsholm
Sumburgh
Sumburgh Head
To Stromness
To Aberdeen

ORKNEY ISLANDS

To Lerwick
North Ronaldsay
Papa Westray
Pierowall
Westray
Westray Firth
Sanday
Rousay
Eday
Egilsay
Stronsay
Mainland
Tingwall
Shapinsay
Orkney
Kirkwall
Stromness
Gritley
Scapa Flow
Hoy
Flotta
St. Margaret's Hope
South Ronaldsay
Burwick
Brough Ness
Pentland Skerries
Dunnet Head
Island of Stroma
John 'o' Groats
Duncansby Head
To Scrabster
Castletown
A9
Sinclair's Bay
Watten
Mybster
A882
Wick
Firth
To Invergordon
To Stromness

Flotta · St
Bu Brou
Pentland Firth
To Stromness
Dunnet Head
Island of Stroma
John 'o' Groats
Dunc Head
Cape Wrath
Strathy Point
Scrabster
Durness
Strathy
Dounreay
Thurso
Castletown
A9
A838
Bettyhill
Halkirk
Watten
Tongue
Strath Halladale
Mybster
A882
Wick
Ben Hope 927
Strathnaver
Caithness
Rhiconich
Laxford Bridge
Forsinard
Scourie
Loch More
Altnaharra
Kinbrace
Latheron
A9
Ulbster
Unapool
Sutherland
A99
ochinyer
Berriedale
Ledmore
Helmsdale
Loch Shin
Helmsdale

Key to Approach Map Symbols

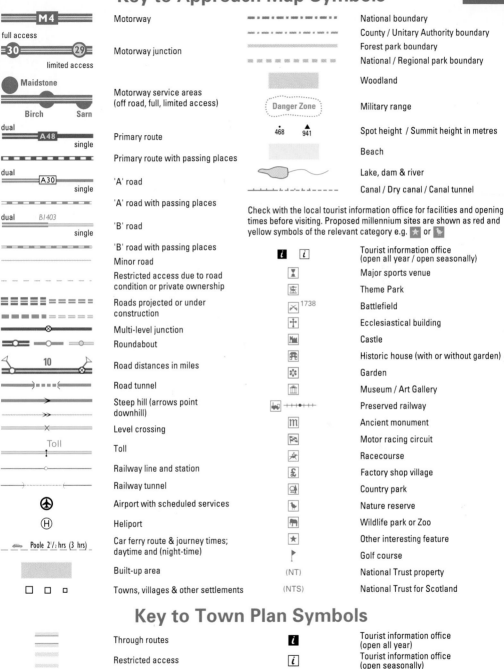

Motorway

Motorway junction

Motorway service areas
(off road, full, limited access)

Primary route

Primary route with passing places

'A' road

'A' road with passing places

'B' road

'B' road with passing places

Minor road

Restricted access due to road condition or private ownership

Roads projected or under construction

Multi-level junction

Roundabout

Road distances in miles

Road tunnel

Steep hill (arrows point downhill)

Level crossing

Toll

Railway line and station

Railway tunnel

Airport with scheduled services

Heliport

Car ferry route & journey times; daytime and (night-time)

Built-up area

Towns, villages & other settlements

National boundary

County / Unitary Authority boundary

Forest park boundary

National / Regional park boundary

Woodland

Military range

Spot height / Summit height in metres

Beach

Lake, dam & river

Canal / Dry canal / Canal tunnel

Check with the local tourist information office for facilities and opening times before visiting. Proposed millennium sites are shown as red and yellow symbols of the relevant category e.g. ⭐ or 🦌

Tourist information office (open all year / open seasonally)

Major sports venue

Theme Park

Battlefield

Ecclesiastical building

Castle

Historic house (with or without garden)

Garden

Museum / Art Gallery

Preserved railway

Ancient monument

Motor racing circuit

Racecourse

Factory shop village

Country park

Nature reserve

Wildlife park or Zoo

Other interesting feature

Golf course

National Trust property

National Trust for Scotland

Key to Town Plan Symbols

Through routes

Restricted access

Pedestrian precinct

Public building

Other important building

Multi-storey / Off-street parking

Tourist information office (open all year)

Tourist information office (open seasonally)

Ecclesiastical building

Railway line

Railway / Light Rail station

Underground station

Metro station (Newcastle)

TOURIST INFORMATION ☎ 01224 632727
ST. NICHOLAS HOUSE, BROAD STREET,
ABERDEEN, AB9 1DE

HOSPITAL A & E ☎ 01224 681818
ABERDEEN ROYAL INFIRMARY, FORESTERHILL,
ABERDEEN, AB25 2ZN

COUNCIL OFFICE ☎ 01224 522000
TOWN HOUSE, BROAD STREET,
ABERDEEN, AB10 1FY

BRISTOL KINGSWOOD

BATH

TROWBRIDGE

Westbury

Frome

Corsham

Melksham

Bradford-on-Avon

Radstock

Midsomer Norton

Keynsham

Clifton

Long Ashton

Bishopsworth

Whitchurch

Knowle

Hanham

Warmley

Cadbury Heath

Oldland

Bitton

Saltford

Corston

Newton St Loe

Bathampton

Batheaston

Bathford

Box

Monkton Farleigh

South Wraxall

Holt

Staverton

Hilperton

North Bradley

Southwick

Rode

Beckington

Frome Market

Warminster Down

Westbury-Leigh

Dilton Marsh

Chapmanslade

Corsley

Upton Scudamore

Bratton

Heywood

Hawkeridge

North Bradley

Trowle Common

Wingfield

Farleigh Hungerford

Tellisford

Lullington

Laverton

Rudge

Berkley

Oldford

Buckland Dinham

Great Elm

Mells

Whatley

Chantry

Vobster

Coleford

Highbury

Holcombe

Kilmersdon

Charlton

Stratton-on-the-Fosse

Downside Abbey

Chilcompton

Ston Easton

Emborough

Binegar

Gurney Slade

Oakhill

Ashwick

Nettlebridge

Leigh upon Mendip

Green Ore

West Horrington

Priddy

Wookey Hole

Easton

Chewton Mendip

Litton

West Harptree

East Harptree

Compton Martin

Ubley

Blagdon

Kewstoke

Nempnett Thrubwell

Regil

Winford

Chew Magna

Chew Stoke

North Widcombe

Bishop Sutton

Chew Valley Lake

Stanton Drew

Stanton Wick

Pensford

Publow

Woollard

Compton Dando

Chelwood

Marksbury

Farmborough

Timsbury

High Littleton

Hallatrow

Paulton

Clutton

Temple Cloud

Cameley

Hinton Blewett

Cholwell

Stowey

Bishop Sutton

Clandown

Welton

Writhlington

Shoscombe

Peasedown St John

Camerton

Carlingcott

Dunkerton

Combe Hay

Midford

Wellow

Norton St Philip

Hinton Priory

Hinton Charterhouse

Stoney Littleton Long Barrow

Faulkland

Hemington

Hardington

Laverton

Woolverton

Lullington

Rode

Beckington

Berkley

Chew Stoke

Priston

Englishcombe

Inglesbatch

Stanton Prior

Burnett

Queen Charlton

Brislington

Longwell Green

Hanham

Warmley

Abson

Doynton

Pennsylvania

Wick

Bridgeyate

Bridge Heath

Oldland

North Stoke

Upton Cheyney

Langridge

Woolley

Charlcombe

Swainswick

Lansdown

Kelston

Weston

Twerton

Odd Down

Combe Down

Monkton Combe

Claverton

Limpley Stoke

Freshford

Westwood

Wingfield

Trowbridge

Southwick

North Bradley

Hawkeridge

Heywood

Warminster

Cold Ashton

Marshfield

St Catherine

Colerne

Ditteridge

Ashley

Monkton Farleigh

Farleigh

Holt

Broughton Gifford

Great Chalfield Manor

Bradford Leigh

Atworth

Neston

Gastard

Hawthorn

Thickwood

Slaughterford

Biddestone

Sheldon Manor

Cross Keys

The Shoe

Upper Wraxall

Shaw

Whitley

Norrington Common

Semington

Seend

Seend Cleeve

Bulkington

Keevil

Steeple Ashton

West Ashton

North Bradley

Yarnbrook

Bratton

Edington

A350 A365 A361 A363 A366 A4 A46 A420 A431 A36 A37 A39 A362 A367 A368 A369 A370 A38 A4175 A4174 A4320 B3109 B3353 B3105 B3108 B3110 B3114 B3115 B3116 B3119 B3124 B3128 B3130 B3133 B3134 B3135 B3136 B3139 B3140 A3098 A3099 B3104 B3106

STD Code 01225

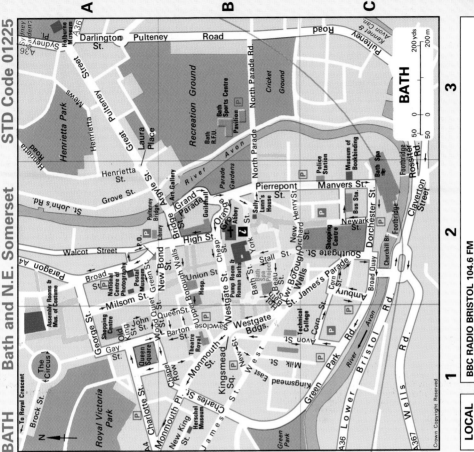

LOCAL RADIO

BBC RADIO BRISTOL 104.6 FM
BRUNEL CLASSIC GOLD 1260 AM, GWR FM 103 FM

TOURIST INFORMATION ☎ 01225 477101
ABBEY CHAMBERS, ABBEY CHURCH YARD,
BATH, BA1 1LY

HOSPITAL A & E ☎ 01225 428331
ROYAL UNITED HOSPITAL, COMBE PARK,
BATH, BA1 3NG

COUNCIL OFFICE ☎ 01225 477000
THE GUILDHALL, HIGH STREET,
BATH, BA1 5AW

BIRMINGHAM West Midlands STD Code 0121

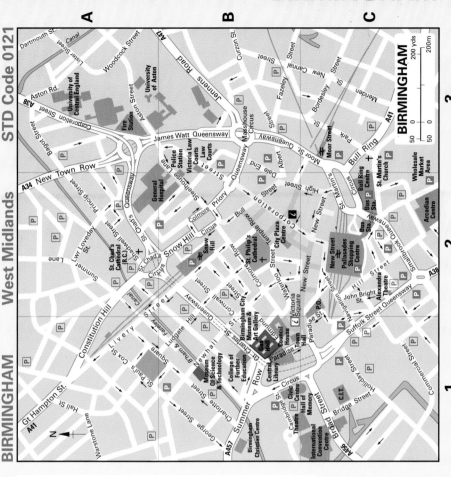

BIRMINGHAM

Scale: 200 yds / 200m

LOCAL RADIO

BBC RADIO WM 95.6 FM
RADIO XL 1296 AM, BRMB 96.4 FM, HEART FM 100.7 FM, GALAXY 102.2 FM

TOURIST INFORMATION ☎ 0121 643 2514
2 CITY ARCADE, BIRMINGHAM,
WEST MIDLANDS, B2 4TX

HOSPITAL A & E ☎ 0121 554 3801
CITY HOSPITAL, DUDLEY ROAD,
BIRMINGHAM, B18 7QH

COUNCIL OFFICE ☎ 0121 303 9944
COUNCIL HOUSE, VICTORIA SQUARE,
BIRMINGHAM, B1 1BB

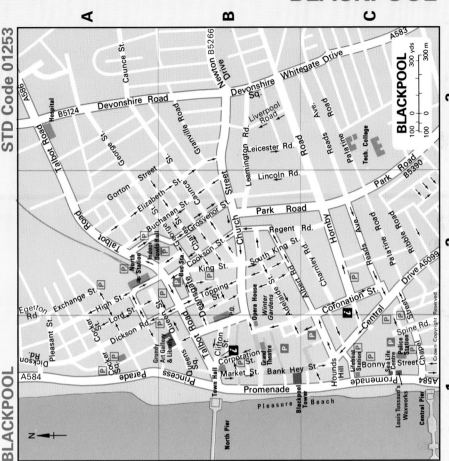

BLACKPOOL

LOCAL RADIO

BBC RADIO LANCASHIRE 104.5 FM
MAGIC 999 AM, THE WAVE FM 96.5 FM, ROCK FM 97.4 FM,

TOURIST INFORMATION ☎ 01253 478222
1 CLIFTON STREET, BLACKPOOL, FY1 1LY

HOSPITAL A & E ☎ 01253 300000
VICTORIA HOSPITAL, WHINNEY HEYS ROAD,
BLACKPOOL, FY3 8NR

COUNCIL OFFICE ☎ 01253 477477
TOWN HALL MUNICIPAL BUILDINGS,
TALBOT SQUARE, BLACKPOOL, FY1 1NB

STD Code 01202

BOURNEMOUTH

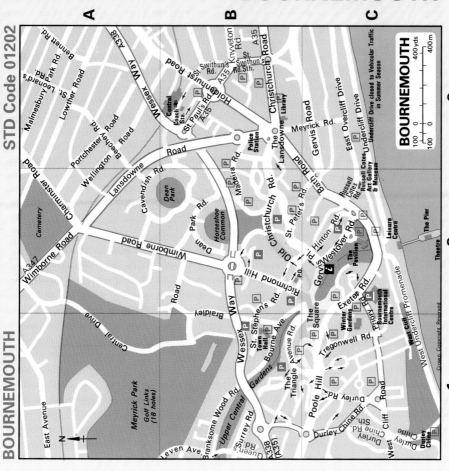

LOCAL RADIO

BBC RADIO SOLENT 96.1 & 103.8 FM
CLASSIC GOLD 828 AM, 2CR FM 102.3 FM, THE NRG 107.6 FM

TOURIST INFORMATION ☎ 0906 802 0234
WESTOVER ROAD, BOURNEMOUTH, BH1 2BU

HOSPITAL A & E ☎ 01202 303626
ROYAL BOURNEMOUTH HOSPITAL,
CASTLE LANE EAST, BOURNEMOUTH, BH7 7DW

COUNCIL OFFICE ☎ 01202 451451
TOWN HALL, BOURNE AVENUE,
BOURNEMOUTH, BH2 6EB

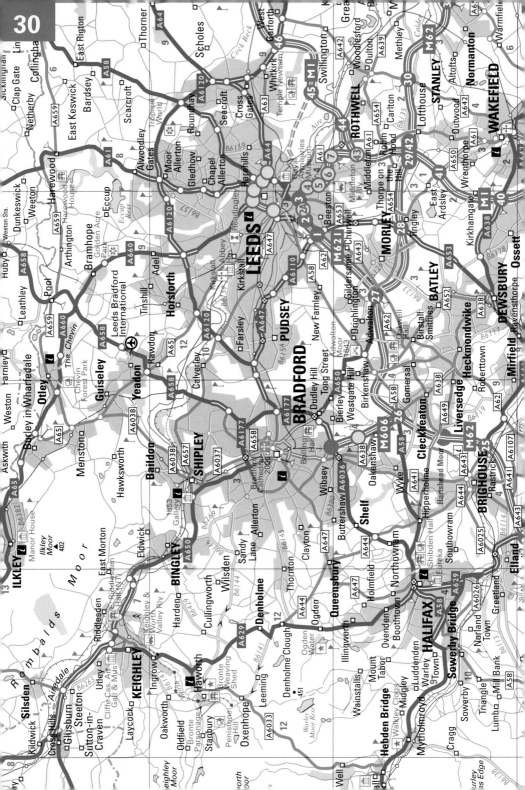

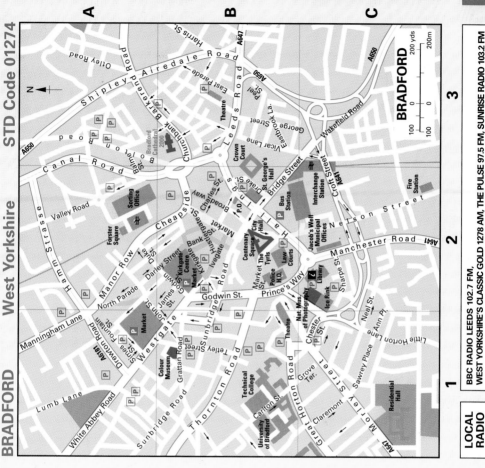

BRADFORD   West Yorkshire   STD Code 01274

LOCAL RADIO

BBC RADIO LEEDS 102.7 FM,
WEST YORKSHIRE'S CLASSIC GOLD 1278 AM, THE PULSE 97.5 FM, SUNRISE RADIO 103.2 FM

TOURIST INFORMATION ☎ 01274 753678
CENTRAL LIBRARY,
PRINCES WAY, BRADFORD, W. YORKS, BD1 1NN

HOSPITAL A & E ☎ 01274 542200
BRADFORD ROYAL INFIRMARY,
DUCKWORTH LANE, BRADFORD, BD9 6RJ

COUNCIL OFFICE ☎ 01274 752111
CITY HALL, CHANNING WAY,
BRADFORD, BD1 1HY

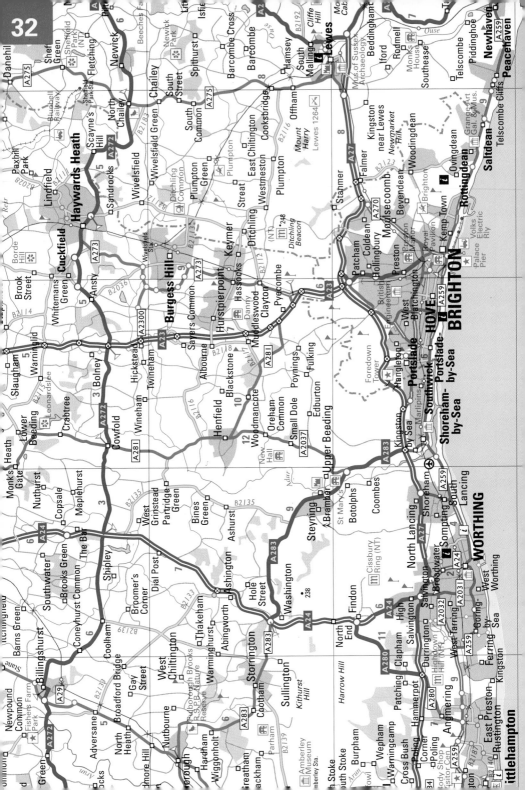

BRIGHTON

Brighton & Hove

STD Code 01273

BRIGHTON

Crown Copyright Reserved

Beaconsfield Villas	A2
Bear Road	A3
Bonchurch Road	B3
Buckingham Road	B2
Cheapside	B2
Church Street	C2
Churchill Square	C2
Clifton Hill	B1
Coombe Road	A3
Davey Drive	A3
Davigdor Road	B1
Dewe Road	A3
Ditchling Rise	A2
Dyke Road	A1
Eastern Road	C3
Edward Street	C2
Elm Grove	B3
Florence Road	A2
Freshfield Road	C3
Gloucester Road	B2
Grand Junction Road	C2
Hartlington Road	B3
Highcroft Villas	A1
Holland Road	B1
Hollingbury Road	A2
Hollingdean Road	A3
Islingword Road	B3
John Street	C2
King's Road	C1
Lansdowne Road	B1
Lewes Road	B3
London Road	B2
Madeira Drive	C2

Marine Parade	C2
Montefiore Road	B1
Montpelier Road	C1
North Street	C2
Old Shoreham Road	B1
Old Steine	C2
Preston Circus	B2
Preston Drive	A2
Preston Park Avenue	A2
Preston Road	A1
Queen's Park Road	B3
Queen's Road	C2
Richmond Place	B2
Richmond Terrace	B2
St. James's Street	C2
Southover Street	B3
South Road	A1
Stanford Avenue	A2
Stanford Road	A1
The Crestway	A3
The Drove	B2
The Lanes	C2
The Upper Drive	A1
Union Road	B1
Upper Hollingdean	A2
Road	
Upper Lewes Road	B2
Upper North Street	C1
Viaduct Road	B2
West Street	C2
Western Road	C1
York Avenue	B1
York Place	B2

TOURIST INFORMATION ☎ 01273 292599
10 BARTHOLOMEW SQUARE,
BRIGHTON, BN1 1JS

HOSPITAL A & E ☎ 01273 696955
ROYAL SUSSEX COUNTY HOSPITAL,
EASTERN ROAD, BRIGHTON, BN2 5BE

COUNCIL OFFICE ☎ 01273 290000
TOWN HALL, BARTHOLOMEWS,
BRIGHTON, BN1 1JA

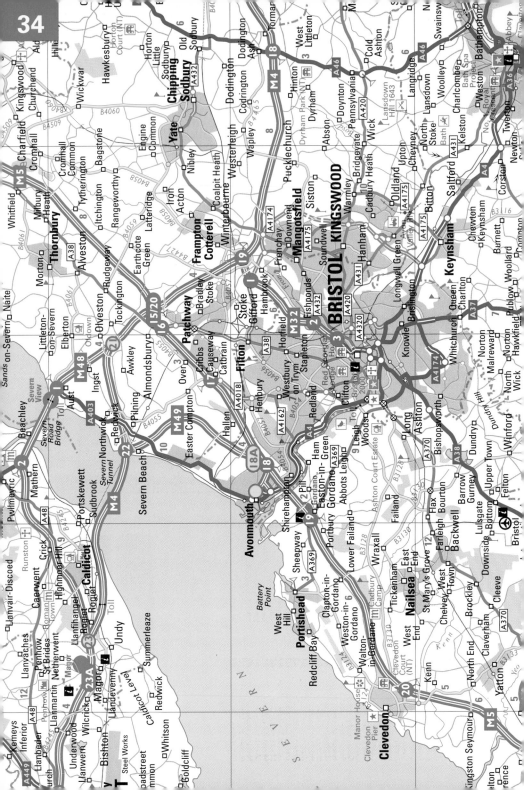

STD Code 0117

BRISTOL

TOURIST INFORMATION ☎ 0117 926 0767
ST. NICHOLAS CHURCH, ST. NICHOLAS STREET,
BRISTOL , BS1 1UE

HOSPITAL A & E ☎ 0117 923 0000
BRISTOL ROYAL INFIRMARY,
MARLBOROUGH STREET, BRISTOL, BS2 8HW

COUNCIL OFFICE ☎ 0117 922 2000
THE COUNCIL HOUSE, COLLEGE GREEN,
BRISTOL, BS1 5TR

LOCAL RADIO

BBC RADIO BRISTOL 95.5 FM
BRUNEL CLASSIC GOLD 1260 AM, GWR FM 96.3 FM, GALAXY 101 FM

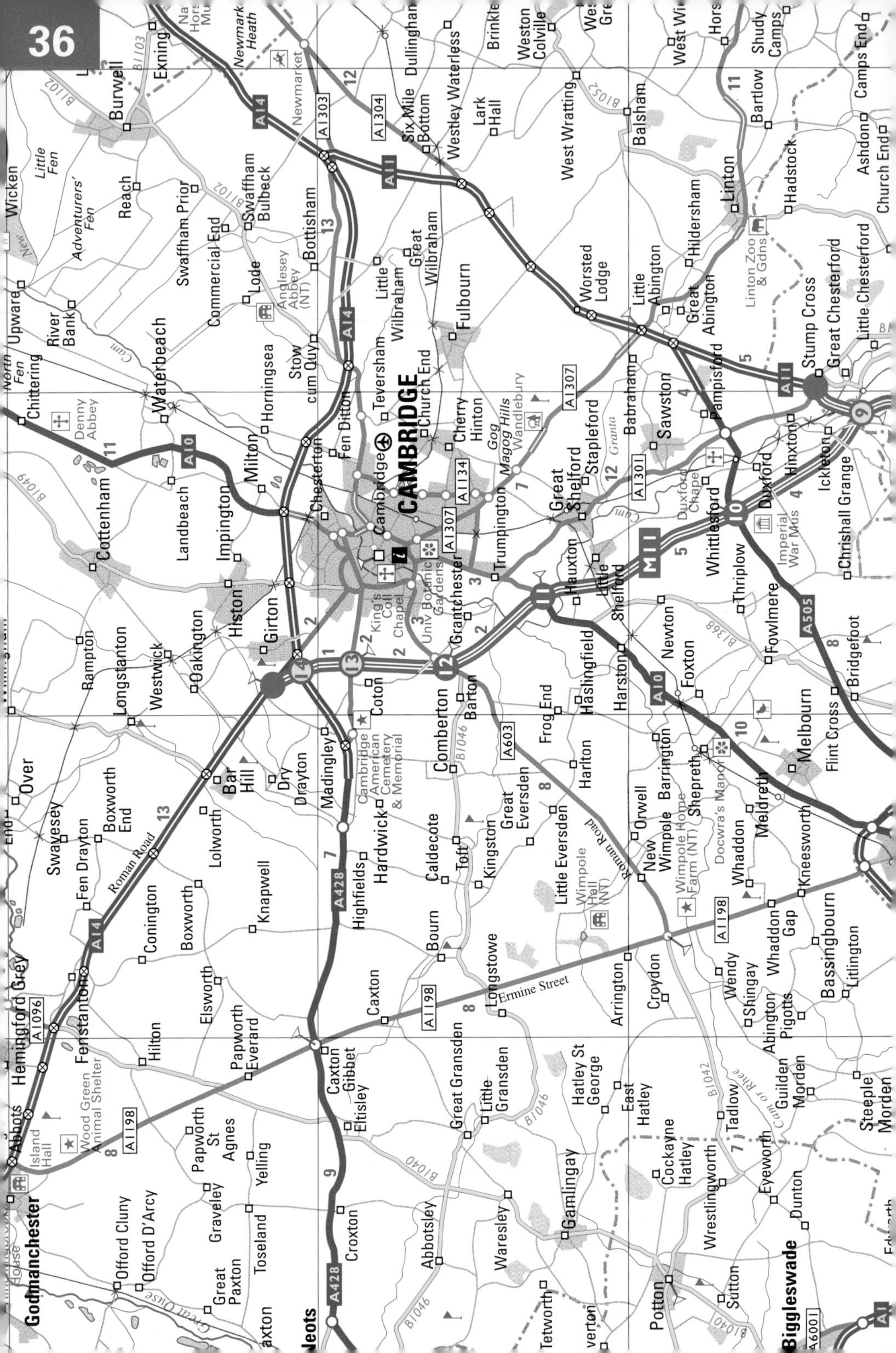
CAMBRIDGE
Cambridge
Chesterton
Fen Ditton
Teversham
Cherry Hinton
Church End
Trumpington
Grantchester
King's Coll Chapel
Univ Botanic Gardens
Girton
Histon
Impington
Milton
Landbeach
Waterbeach
Cottenham
Oakington
Westwick
Rampton
Longstanton
Willingham
Over
Swavesey
Fen Drayton
Boxworth End
Bar Hill
Dry Drayton
Lolworth
Madingley
Coton
Cambridge American Cemetery & Memorial
Hardwick
Highfields
Comberton
Barton
Caldecote
Toft
Kingston
Great Eversden
Little Eversden
Harlton
Haslingfield
Frog End
Harston
Hauxton
Little Shelford
Great Shelford
Stapleford
Newton
Foxton
Barrington
Shepreth
Orwell
New Wimpole
Wimpole Hall (NT)
Wimpole Home Farm (NT)
Docwra's Manor
Meldreth
Melbourn
Whaddon
Kneesworth
Bassingbourn
Litlington
Royston
Thriplow
Fowlmere
Whittlesford
Duxford
Imperial War Mus
Duxford Chapel
Hinxton
Ickleton
Chrishall Grange
Sawston
Pampisford
Babraham
Great Abington
Little Abington
Hildersham
Linton
Linton Zoo & Gdns
Hadstock
Bartlow
Ashdon
Church End
Stump Cross
Great Chesterford
Little Chesterford
Worsted Lodge
Fulbourn
Great Wilbraham
Little Wilbraham
Magog Hills
Wandlebury
Gog
Balsham
West Wratting
Weston Colville
West Wickham
Westley Waterless
Six Mile Bottom
Dullingham
Brinkley
Lark Hall
Newmarket
Newmarket Heath
Exning
Burwell
Reach
Swaffham Prior
Swaffham Bulbeck
Commercial End
Lode
Anglesey Abbey (NT)
Bottisham
Stow cum Quy
Horningsea
Upware
River Bank
Wicken
Little Fen
Adventurers' Fen
Chittering
Denny Abbey
Horseheath
Shudy Camps
Camps End
Knapwell
Boxworth
Conington
Elsworth
Fenstanton
Hilton
Hemingford Grey
Hemingford Abbots
Godmanchester
Island Hall
Wood Green Animal Shelter
Papworth Everard
Papworth St Agnes
Yelling
Graveley
Offord Cluny
Offord D'Arcy
Toseland
Great Paxton
Caxton
Caxton Gibbet
Eltisley
Croxton
Abbotsley
Bourn
Longstowe
Great Gransden
Little Gransden
Waresley
Gamlingay
Hatley St George
East Hatley
Cockayne Hatley
Arrington
Croydon
Wendy
Shingay
Abington Pigotts
Whaddon Gap
Guilden Morden
Steeple Morden
Tadlow
Wrestlingworth
Eyeworth
Dunton
Potton
Sutton
Biggleswade
Tetworth
Roman Road
Ermine Street
Great Ouse
Cam
Cam or Rhee
Granta
A14
A11
A10
A505
A603
A428
A1198
A1303
A1304
A1307
A1134
A1301
A1096
A1
A6001
M11
B1102
B1103
B1049
B1052
B1368
B1046
B1042
B1040

CAMBRIDGE · Cambridgeshire · STD Code 01223

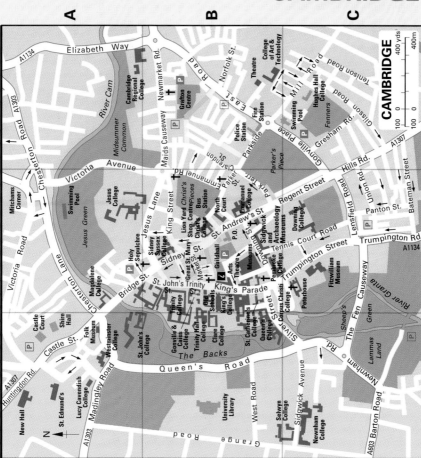

CAMBRIDGE

LOCAL RADIO

BBC RADIO CAMBRIDGESHIRE 96 FM
Q 103 FM, CAMBRIDGE RED 107.9 FM

TOURIST INFORMATION ☎ 01223 322640
WHEELER STREET, CAMBRIDGE,
CAMBRIDGESHIRE, CB2 3QB

HOSPITAL A & E ☎ 01223 245151
ADDENBROOKE'S HOSPITAL, HILLS ROAD,
CAMBRIDGE, CB2 2QQ

COUNCIL OFFICE ☎ 01223 457000
THE GUILDHALL, MARKET SQUARE,
CAMBRIDGE, CB2 3QJ

MARGATE

Westgate on Sea

HERNE BAY

WHITSTABLE

CANTERBURY

Isle of Thanet

Sandwich Bay

Pegwell Bay

Sandwich Flats

SANDWICH

Minster

Manston

RAF Manston

St Augustine's Cross

Cliffs End

Acol

Birchington

Monkton

Gore Street

Sarre

St Nicholas at Wade

West Stourmouth

East Stourmouth

Westmarsh

Ware

Cop Street

Ash

Marshborough

Woodnesborough

Worth

Hacklinge

Sholden

Northbourne

Betteshanger

Great Mongeham

Ripple

Sutton

Ashley

West Langdon

East Langdon

Guston

Whitfield

West Studdal

East Studdal

Martin Mill Sta.

Eastry

Knowlton

Eastling

Goodnestone

Chillenden

Nonington

Easole Street

Shepherdswell or Sibertswold

Coldred

Barfreston

Eythorne

Elvington

Tilmanstone

Temple Ewell

Lydden

Wootton

Selstead

Denton

Womenswold

Wollage Green

Wingham

Staple

Marshborough

Bramling

Bekesbourne

Patrixbourne

Adisham

Barham

Kingston

Derringstone

Bishopsbourne

Lower Hardres

Nackington

Bridge

Street End

Upper Hardres Court

Petham

Waltham

Bossingham

Stelling Minnis

Sixmile Cottages

Elham

Lyminge

Bladbean

Wingmore

Breach

Lyminge Forest

Stone Street

Bodsham Green

Hastingleigh

Lymbridge Green

Wye

Brook

ASHFORD

Kennington

Boughton Aluph

Eastwell Park

Boughton Lees

Challock

Molash

Godmersham

Chilham

Chilham Castle

Crundale

Bilting

Sole Street

Hassell Street

Westwell

Charing

Westwell Leacon

Stalisfield Green

Throwley

Eastling

Frith

Sheldwich

Badlesmere

Leaveland

Selling

Shottenden

Chilham

Old Wives Lees

Shalmsford Street

Chartham Hatch

Chartham

Thanington

Harbledown

Rough Common

Blean

Honey Hill

Pean Hill

Tyler Hill

Broad Oak

Sturry

Fordwich

Littlebourne

Ickham

Wickhambreaux

Stodmarsh

Preston

Stourmouth

Grove

Chislet

Marshside

Upstreet

Hoath

Maypole

Herne Common

Calcott

Hunters Forstal

Highstead

Broomfield

Boyden Gate

Hillborough

Beltinge

Reculver

Swalecliffe

Chestfield

Seasalter

Graveney

Goodnestone

Hernhill

Dargate

Yorkletts

Dunkirk

Boughton Street

Overland

Dunkirk

Whitehill

Throwley

Faversham

Oare

Uplees

Preston

Ospringe

North Street

Luddenham Court

Conyer

Teynham Sta.

Lynsted

WARDEN

Leysdown-on-Sea

Eastchurch

ISLE OF SHEPPEY

Isle of Harty

Eastchurch Marshes

Shell Ness

Swale

Minster

Brogdale Horticultural Trust

Chartham Castle

A253

A256

A257

A258

A28

A299

A290

A291

A2

A2050

A252

A251

A260

A2070

B2046

B2068

B2205

M2

M20

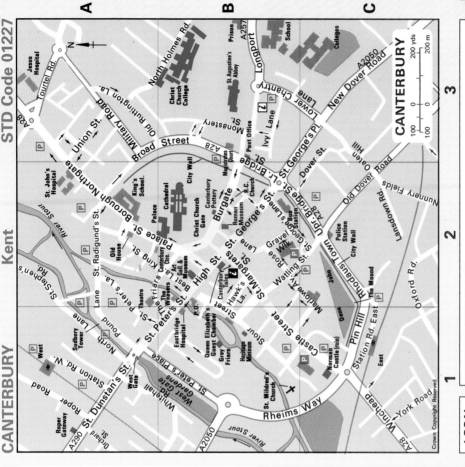

CANTERBURY

Best Lane	B2	Pin Hill	C1
Borough Northgate	A2	Pound Lane	A1
Broad Street	A3	Rheims Way	B1
Burgate	B2	Rhodaus Town	B2
Castle Street	C1	Roper Road	A1
Dover Street	C2	Rose Lane	B2
Gravel Walk	B2	St. Dunstan's Street	A1
Hawk's Lane	B2	St. George's Lane	C2
High Street	B2	St. George's Place	B2
Ivy Lane	B3	St. George's Street	B2
King Street	A2	St. Margarets Street	B2
Lansdown Road	C2	St. Peter's Lane	A1
Longport	B2	St. Peter's Place	B1
Lower Bridge Street	B2	St. Peter's Street	A1
Lower Chantry Lane	C2	St. Radigund's Street	A2
Marlowe Avenue	C2	St. Stephen's Road	A2
Military Road	A3	Station Road East	C1
Monastery Street	B3	Station Road West	A1
New Dover Road	C3	Stour Street	B1
North Holmes Road	A3	The Friar's	A2
North Lane	A1	Tourtel Road	A3
Nunnery Fields	C2	Union Street	C2
Oaten Hill	C2	Upper Bridge Street	B2
Old Dover Road	B2	Watling Street	B2
Old Ruttington Lane	A3	Whitehall Road	B1
Orchard Street	A1	Wincheap	C1
Oxford Road	C2	York Road	C1
Palace Street	B2		

TOURIST INFORMATION ☎ 01227 766567
34 ST. MARGARET'S STREET, CANTERBURY,
KENT, CT1 2TG

HOSPITAL A & E ☎ 01227 766877
KENT & CANTERBURY HOSPITAL,
ETHELBERT ROAD, CANTERBURY, CT1 3NG

COUNCIL OFFICE ☎ 01227 862000
COUNCIL OFFICES, MILITARY ROAD,
CANTERBURY, CT1 1YW

CARDIFF

STD Code 029

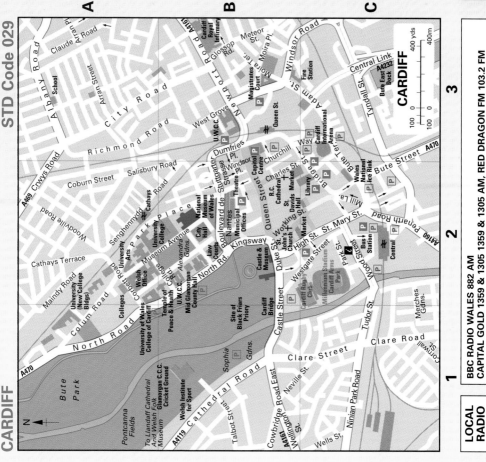

LOCAL RADIO

BBC RADIO WALES 882 AM
CAPITAL GOLD 1359 & 1305 1359 & 1305 AM, RED DRAGON FM 103.2 FM

TOURIST INFORMATION ☎ 029 2022 7281
CARDIFF VISITOR CENTRE,
16 WOOD STREET, CARDIFF, CF10 1ES

HOSPITAL A & E ☎ 029 2074 7747
CARDIFF UNIVERSITY OF WALES HOSPITAL,
HEATH PARK, CARDIFF, CF14 4XW

COUNCIL OFFICE ☎ 029 2087 2000
COUNTY HALL, ATLANTIC WHARF,
CARDIFF, CF10 4UW

Three Counties Showground
Welland
A4101
Upton upon Severn
Little Welland
Hollybush
Castlemorton
Birts Street
Camer's Green
Longdon
Sledge Green
Pendock
A438
Eldersfield
Chaceley
Corse Lawn
Deerhurst
Staunton
Snig's End
Hasfield
Tirley
Nup End White End
Ashleworth
Ashleworth Tithe Barn (NT)
Hartpury
Highleadon
Sandhurst
Nature in Art
Norton
Down Hatherley
Staverton
Staverton Bridge
Twigworth
Maisemore
Lassington
Longford
Gloucestershire
Innsworth
Highnam
A40
A48
Hempsted
Elmore Back
Elmore
Quedgeley
Hardwicke
Tuffley
Whaddon
Brookthorpe
M5
A38
Moreton Valence
Harescombe
Haresfield
Edge
Pitchcombe
Stroud Green
Whiteshill
Randwick
Stonehouse
A419
Eastington
Leonard Stanley
King's Stanley
Frocester
Woodchester
Coaley
St. Leonards Priory
Thrupp
Brimscombe
Amberley
Hyde
Chalford
Frampton Mansell
Sapperton
Oakridge Lynch
Bussage
Eastcombe
Bournes Green
Bisley
Edgeworth
Sudgrove
Duntisbourne Abbots
Duntisbourne Leer
Duntisbourne Rouse
Daglingworth
Baunton
Stratton
Cirencester
Corinium
A419
A429

Naunton
Stratford
Ripple
Uckinghall
Twyning Green
Twyning
Shuthonger
Bushley
The Mythe
Forthampton
Tewkesbury
Tewkesbury 1471
Abbey
Apperley
Odda's Chapel
Lower Apperley
Coombe Hill
Leigh
Boddington
Hardwicke
Stoke Orchard
Elmstone Hardwicke
Uckington
Swindon Village
Cheltenham
Golden Valley
A4013
A4019
Up Hatherley
Leckhampton
Badgeworth
Shurdington
Bentham
Crickley Hill
Churchdown
Barnwood
Hucclecote
Brockworth
Matson
Upton St Leonards
Robinswood Hill
Little Witcombe
Great Witcombe
Pinknash Abbey
Prinknash Park
Pottery
Rococo
Cranham
Sheepscombe
Painswick
The Camp
Whiteway
Slad
Miserden
Misarden Park Gardens
Winstone
Syde
Stroud
Rodborough
Bussage

Hanley Castle
Baughton
Holly Green
Eckington
Strensham
Bredon's Norton
Naunton
A38
M50
Twyning
Bredon's Hardwick
Bredon
Northway
Aston Cross
Pamington
Ashchurch
Walton Cardiff
Fiddington
Tredington
Northway
Great Comberton
Bricklehampton (ruins)
A46
Netherton
Bredon Hill 293
Elmley Castle
Hinton on the Green
Ashton under Hill
Sedgeberrow
Kemerton
Overbury
Conderton
Beckford
Great Washbourne
Alderton
Toddington
New Town
Dumbleton
Oxenton
Dixton
Gretton
Greet
Langley Hill
Winchcombe
Cleeve Hill
Roman Villa
Sudeley
Belas Knap Long Ba
Bishop's Cleeve
Woodmancote
Southam
Prestbury
Charlton Abb
Sevenhampton
Brock
CHELTENHAM
Whittington
Dowdeswell
Syreford
Andoversfor
Charlton Kings
Pilley
Kilkenny
Foxcote
Ship
Seven Springs
Ullenwood
Coberley
Cowley
Upper Coberley
Withing
Withington Woods
Chedwo
Roman V
Chedwo
Colesbourne
Birdlip
Brimpsfield
Elkstone
A417
Roman Road
Ermin Way
A435
Rendcomb
Woodmancote
Calmsden
North Cerney
Bagendon
Syde

A46
A434
M5
A4173
A4008
B4066

Gotherington
223
Cheltenham
330
295
297
Roman Villa
m

CHELTENHAM

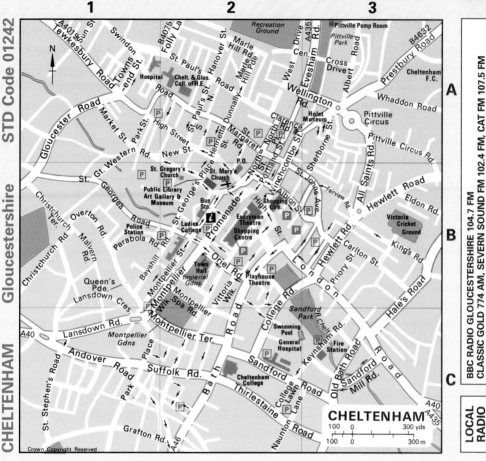

TOURIST INFORMATION ☎ 01242 522878
77 THE PROMENADE, CHELTENHAM,
GLOUCESTERSHIRE, GL50 1PP

HOSPITAL A & E ☎ 01242 222222
CHELTENHAM GENERAL HOSPITAL,
SANDFORD ROAD, CHELTENHAM, GL53 7AN

COUNCIL OFFICE ☎ 01242 261801
MUNICIPAL OFFICES, THE PROMENADE,
CHELTENHAM, GL50 1PP

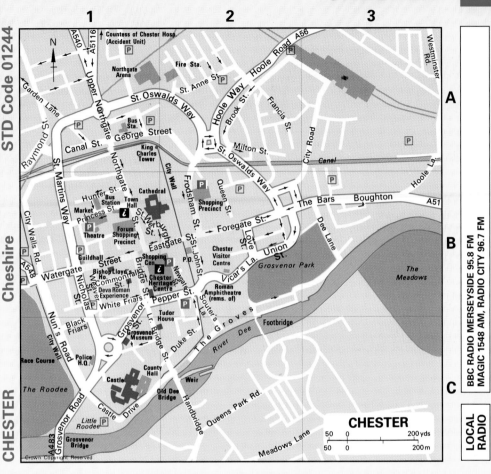

CHESTER

Scale: 50 0 200 yds / 50 0 200 m

STD Code 01244

Cheshire

CHESTER

Crown Copyright Reserved

BBC RADIO MERSEYSIDE 95.8 FM
MAGIC 1548 AM, RADIO CITY 96.7 FM

LOCAL RADIO

TOURIST INFORMATION ☎ 01244 402111
TOWN HALL, NORTHGATE STREET,
CHESTER, CHESHIRE, CH1 2HJ

HOSPITAL A & E ☎ 01244 365000
COUNTESS OF CHESTER HOSPITAL, HEALTH PK,
LIVERPOOL ROAD, CHESTER, CH2 1UL

COUNCIL OFFICE ☎ 01244 324324
TOWN HALL, MARKET SQUARE,
NORTHGATE STREET, CHESTER, CH1 2HJ

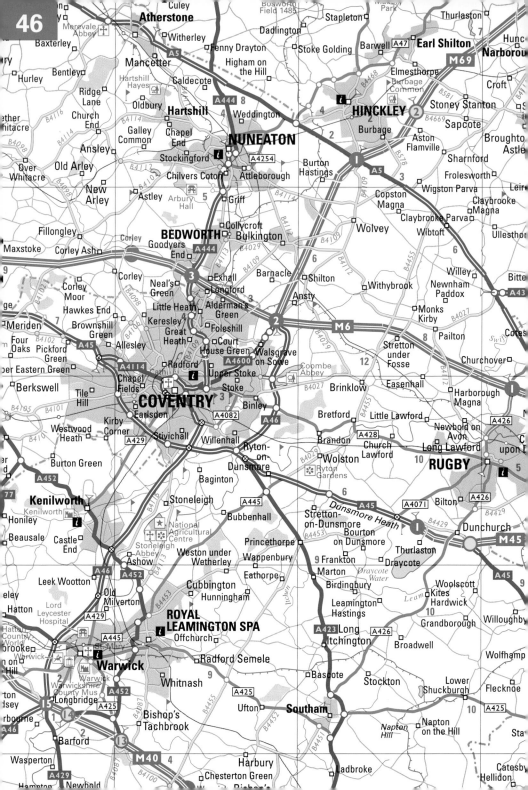

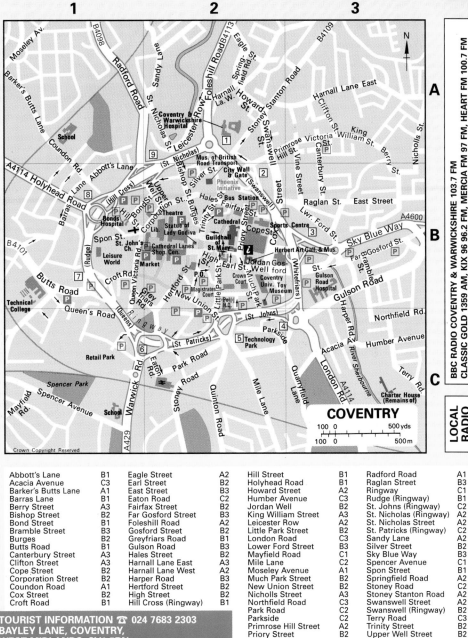

COVENTRY

Abbott's Lane	B1	Eagle Street	A2	Hill Street	B1	Radford Road	A1
Acacia Avenue	C3	Earl Street	B2	Holyhead Road	B1	Raglan Street	B3
Barker's Butts Lane	A1	East Street	B3	Howard Street	A2	Ringway	C1
Barras Lane	B1	Eaton Road	C2	Humber Avenue	C3	Rudge (Ringway)	B1
Berry Street	A3	Fairfax Street	B2	Jordan Well	B2	St. Johns (Ringway)	C2
Bishop Street	B2	Far Gosford Street	B3	King William Street	A3	St. Nicholas (Ringway)	A2
Bond Street	B1	Foleshill Road	A2	Leicester Row	A2	St. Nicholas Street	A2
Bramble Street	B3	Gosford Street	B2	Little Park Street	B2	St. Patricks (Ringway)	C2
Burges	B2	Greyfriars Road	B1	London Road	C3	Sandy Lane	A2
Butts Road	B1	Gulson Road	B3	Lower Ford Street	B3	Silver Street	B2
Canterbury Street	A3	Hales Street	B2	Mayfield Road	C1	Sky Blue Way	B3
Clifton Street	A3	Harnall Lane East	A3	Mile Lane	C2	Spencer Avenue	C1
Cope Street	B2	Harnall Lane West	A2	Moseley Avenue	A1	Spon Street	B1
Corporation Street	B2	Harper Road	B3	Much Park Street	B2	Springfield Road	A2
Coundon Road	A1	Hertford Street	B2	New Union Street	B2	Stoney Road	C2
Cox Street	B2	High Street	B2	Nicholls Street	A3	Stoney Stanton Road	A2
Croft Road	B1	Hill Cross (Ringway)	B1	Northfield Road	C3	Swanswell Street	A2
				Park Road	C2	Swanswell (Ringway)	B2
				Parkside	C2	Terry Road	C3
				Primrose Hill Street	A2	Trinity Street	B2
				Priory Street	B2	Upper Well Street	B2
				Quarryfield Lane	C3	Victoria Street	A3
				Queens (Ringway)	C1	Vine Street	A3
				Queen's Road	B1	Warwick Road	C1
				Queen Victoria Road	B1	Whitefriars (Ringway)	B3
				Quinton Road	C2		

TOURIST INFORMATION ☎ 024 7683 2303
BAYLEY LANE, COVENTRY,
WEST MIDLANDS, CV1 5RN

HOSPITAL A & E ☎ 024 7622 4055
COVENTRY & WARWICKSHIRE HOSPITAL,
STONEY STANTON ROAD, COVENTRY, CV1 4FH

COUNCIL OFFICE ☎ 024 7683 3333
COUNCIL HOUSE, EARL STREET,
COVENTRY, CV1 5RR

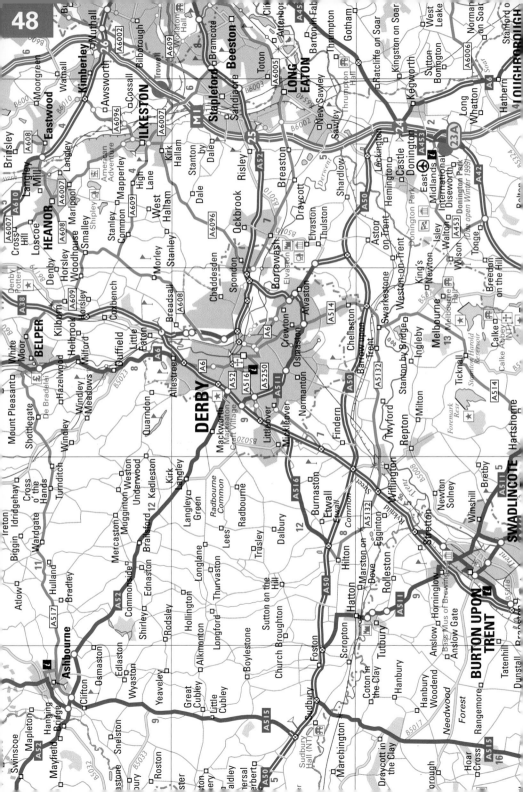

DERBY

STD Code 01332

Abbey Street	C1
Albert Street	B2
Arthur Street	A1
Babington Lane	C2
Becket Street	B1
Bold Lane	B1
Bradshaw Way	C2
Bridge Street	A1
Burton Road	C1
Canal Street	C3
City Road	A2
Clarke Street	A3
Corporation Street	B2
Curzon Street	B1
Darley Lane	A2
Derwent Street	B2
Drewry Lane	C1
Duffield Road	A1
Eastgate	B3
East Street	B2
Edward Street	A1
Exeter Street	B2
Ford Street	B1
Fox Street	A3
Friar Gate	B1
Friary Street	B1
Full Street	B2
Gerard Street	C1
Gower Street	C2
Green Lane	C2
Handyside Street	A2
Iron Gate	B2
Kedleston Road	A1
King Street	A1
Liversage Street	C3
Lodge Lane	A1
London Road	C2
Macklin Street	B1
Mansfield Road	A2
Market Place	B2
Meadow Road	B3
Monk Street	C1
Morledge	B2
Normanton Road	C1
North Street	A1
Nottingham Road	A3
Osmaston Road	C2
Queen Street	B1
Sacheverel Street	A2
St. Alkmunds Way	A2
St. Helen's Street	A1
St. Mary's Gate	B1
St. Peter's Church Yard	C2
St. Peter's Street	B2
Sir Frank Whittle Road	A3
Sitwell Street	C2
Stafford Street	B1
Station Approach	B3
Stockbrook Street	C1
Stores Road	A3
Traffic Street	C2
Uttoxeter New Road	B1
Victoria Street	B2
Wardwick	B1
Willow Row	A2
Wilson Street	B2
Woods Lane	C1

LOCAL RADIO

BBC RADIO DERBY 94.8 FM
CLASSIC GOLD GEM 945 AM, RAM FM 102.8 FM

TOURIST INFORMATION ☎ 01332 255802
ASSEMBLY ROOMS, MARKET PLACE,
DERBY, DE1 3AH

HOSPITAL A & E ☎ 01332 347141
DERBYSHIRE ROYAL INFIRMARY,
LONDON ROAD, DERBY, DE1 2QY

COUNCIL OFFICE ☎ 01332 293111
THE COUNCIL HOUSE, CORPORATION STREET,
DERBY, DE1 2FS

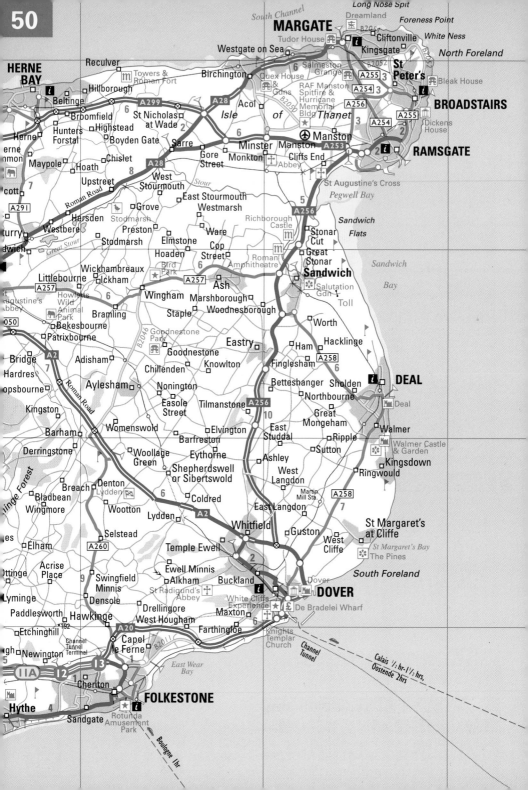

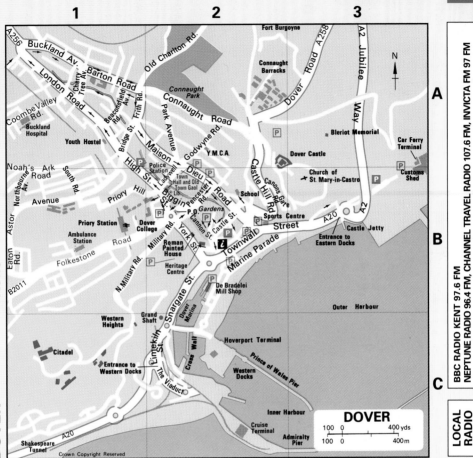

DOVER

100	0			400 yds	
100	0			400 m	

STD Code 01304 · Kent · DOVER

BBC RADIO KENT 97.6 FM
NEPTUNE RADIO 96.4 FM, CHANNEL TRAVEL RADIO 107.6 FM, INVICTA FM 97 FM

LOCAL RADIO

Astor Avenue	B1	Castle Street	B2	Jubilee Way	A3	Old Charlton Road	A2
Barton Road	A1	Cherry Tree Avenue	A1	Ladywell	B2	Park Avenue	A2
Beaconsfield Avenue	A1	Connaught Road	A2	Limekiln Street	C2	Pencester Road	B2
Beaconsfield Road	A1	Coombe Valley Road	A1	London Road	A1	Priory Hill	B1
Biggin Street	B2	Dover Road	A3	Maison Dieu Road	A2	Snargate Street	C2
Bridge Street	A1	Eaton Road	B1	Marine Parade	B2	South Road	B1
Buckland Avenue	A1	Folkestone Road	B1	Military Road	B2	The Viaduct	C2
Cannon Street	B2	Frith Road	A1	Noah's Ark Road	A1	Townwall Street	B2
Canons Gate Road	B2	Godwyne Road	A2	Northbourne Avenue	B1	York Street	B2
Castle Hill Road	B1	High Street	A1	North Military Road	B1		

TOURIST INFORMATION ☎ 01304 205108
TOWNWALL STREET, DOVER, KENT, CT16 1JR

HOSPITAL A & E ☎ 01304 201624
BUCKLAND HOSPITAL, COOMBE VALLEY ROAD,
BUCKLAND, DOVER, CT17 OHD

COUNCIL OFFICE ☎ 01304 821199
COUNCIL OFFICES, WHITE CLIFFS BUSINESS
PARK, DOVER, CT16 3PG

Denbe
Re
Guynd
Arb
Ea
K
Carmyllie
Guynd
Mosston
Denhead
Carnoustie
Bonnington
Sa
Mu
Panbride
Lochlair
Greystone
Carmyllie
Bonnington
Lochlair
Hayhillock
Kirkbuddo
Greenburn
Crombie Mill
Upper Muirdrum
Kirkton of Monikie
Barry Mill (NTS)
Buddon Ness
Whigstreet
Buddo
Inverarity
Carrot
Affleck Affleck
Craigton
Newbigging
Mains of Ardestie
Buddon
Barry Links
Monifieth
Monikie
Greenburn
Laws
Barry
Carrot Hill
Wellbank
Bucklerheads
Drumsturdy
Newbigging
Broughty Ferry
Tentsmuir Point
St Andrews
British Andrews Golf Museum Bay
Gallowfauld
Todhills
Newbigging East March
Burnside of Duntrune
Douglas and Angus
Baldovie
Baldragan
Murroes
Kellas
Broughty
Tayport
Newport-on-Tay
Out Head
Guardbridge
Kincaple
Kincaldrum
Gateside
Balgray
Kirkton of Tealing
Downfield
Tay Road Bridge
Discovery Point & R.R.S. Discovery
Woodhaven
Wormit
Pickletillem
Carrick
Leuchars
Earlshall
RAF Memorial
Kirkton of Strathmartine
Dovecot & Earth House
Clatto
Downfield
Dundee Contemporary
DUNDEE
Tay Bridge
Kirkton
Bottomcraig
Gauldry
Forret Hill
Lucklawhill
Balmullo Logie
Dairsie or Osnaburgh
Ogilvy
Gallow Hill
Craigowl Hill
455
Kirkton of Auchterhouse
Leoch
Muirhead
Lochee
Denhead
Kingoodie
Invergowrie
Abbey (NTS)
Balmerino
Hazelton Walls
Creich
Craigsanquhar
Moonzie
Cairney Lodge
Eassie and Nevay
Nether Handwick
Kinpurney Hill
Auchterhouse Hill
Bonnyton
Auchterhouse
Dronley
Birkhill
Liff Camperdown
Benvie
Longforgan
Coultra
Brunton
Luthrie
Balhelvie
Lindifferon
Meigle
Balkeerie
Kirkinch
Newbigging Newtyle
Thriepley
Lundie
Fowlis
Knapp
Inchture
Grange
Dog Bank
Norman's Law 285
Norman's Hill
Carthagena Bank
Glenduckie Hill
Dunbog
Leitfie
Kinloch
Arthurstone
Ardler
Keillor
Littleton
Blacklaw Hill
Abernyte
Ballindean
Craigdallie
Errol
Port Allen
Glenduckie
Lindores
Hallyburton Forest
King's Seat
Pitmiddle Wood
Kinnaird
Rait
Kilspindie
Mugdrum Island
Lindores Abbey
Newburgh
Rosemount
Markethill
Kettins
Leys
Pitcur
Saucher
Collace
Kirkton of Collace
Kilspindie
Pitroddie
Glendoick
Glencarse
Inchyra
Chapelhill
Pole Hill
Ormiston Hill
Blairgowrie
Coupar Angus
Campmuir
Burrelton
Springfield
Kinrossie
Kinfauns Forest
Woodside
Whitefield
Saucher

Firth of Tay

Braes o the Carse

Carse of Gowrie

A90 · A92 · A94 · A85 · A91 · A914 · A919 · A923 · A928 · A930 · A984 · A913

Tentsmuir Forest

DUNDEE

STD Code 01382

Crown Copyright Reserved

LOCAL RADIO

BBC RADIO SCOTLAND 810 AM/92.4-94.7 FM
RADIO TAY AM 1161 AM, DISCOVERY 102 102 FM, TAY FM 102.8 FM

TOURIST INFORMATION ☎ 01382 527527
7-21 CASTLE STREET, DUNDEE, DD1 3BA

HOSPITAL A & E ☎ 01382 660111
NINEWELLS HOSPITAL, NINEWELLS ROAD,
DUNDEE, DD1 9SY

COUNCIL OFFICE ☎ 01382 434000
CITY CHAMBERS, 21 CITY SQUARE,
DUNDEE, DD1 3BY

SEAHAM
Nose's Point
Easington Colliery
Turning
Horden
Peterlee
Blackhall
Hesleden
Sheraton
Elwick
Crookfoot Resr
Hendon
Ryhope
New Silksworth
Silksworth
Seaton
Dalton-le-Dale
Cold Hesledon
Hawthorn
Easington
Little Thorpe
Shotton
Castle Eden
Hutton Henry
Shotton Colliery
Station Town
South Wingate
Wingate
Wheatley Hill
Trimdon Colliery
Trimdon Grange
Hurworth Burn Resr
Skerne
Fishburn
Sedgefield
Murton
South Hetton
HOUGHTON LE SPRING
Hetton-le-Hole
Easington Lane
Haswell
Ludworth
Thornley
Quarrington Hill
Kelloe
Trimdon
Bishop Middleham
Hardwick Hall
WASHINGTON
Penshaw
Herrington
Fatfield
Shiney Row
Bournmoor
Fence Houses
Colliery Row
East Rainton
West Rainton
Pittington
Littletown
Sherburn
Shadforth
Cassop
Coxhoe
Carrville
Shincliffe
Bowburn
Cornforth
Ferryhill
Chilton
Rushyford
Ouston
Pelton
Great Lumley
Lumley
Finchale
Framwellgate Moor
Cathedral
Botanic Garden
Hett
Dean Bank
Kirk Merrington
Coundon
Coundon Grange
Newfield
CHESTER-LE-STREET
Waldridge Fell
Waldridge
Plawsworth
Kimblesworth
Pity Me
DURHAM
Neville's Cross 1346
Sunderland Bridge
Croxdale
Tudhoe
Spennymoor
Brandon to Bishop Auckland Walk
Beamish
Beamish Open Air Museum
Edmondsley
Sacriston
Witton Gilbert
Bearpark
Langley Moor
Brandon
Browney
Byers Green
Middlestone Moor
Westerton
Bishop Auckland
Grange Villa
Craghead
Holmside
Ushaw Moor
Esh Winning
Brancepeth
Willington
Newfield
Hunwick
Tanfield
Tantobie
STANLEY
South Moor
Maiden Law
Burnhope
Lanchester Valley Walk
Langley Park
Esh
Quebec
Deerness Valley Walk
Oakenshaw
Witton Park
Etherley
Annfield Plain
Consett & Sunderland Rly Path
Hobson
Greencroft Hall
Lanchester
Cornsay Colliery
Waterhouses
East Hedleyhope
Billy Row
Crook
Howden-le-Wear
High Grange
Low Etherley
High Etherley
Derwent Walk
Medomsley
Dipton
Leadgate
Iveston
Cornsay
Fir Tree
Witton-le-Wear
Ebchester
Delves
Satley
Butsfield
Tow Law
Sunniside
Thornley
Hamsterley
Morley
CONSETT
Knitsley
Bedburn
Knitsley Fell
Newlands
Shotley Bridge
Shotleyfield
Carterway Heads
Castleside
Rowley
Allensford
Tunstall Resr
Wolsingham
St John's
Low Redford
Bedburn Beck
Hamsterley Forest
Harvey Hill
Wear
Toll
A19
A179
A182
A1018
A690
A183
A182
A195
A1(M)
A181
A177
A688
A689
A167
A693
A691
A692
A6076
A694
A68
B1281
B1320
B1283
B1432
B1287
B1280
B1286
B1404
B1285
B1284
B1279
B1278
B6291
B6300
B6302
B6313
B6532
B6168
B6301
B6296
B6299
B6297
B6286
B6287
B6288
B6282
B6278
B6310
64
63
62
61
60

STD Code 0191

DURHAM

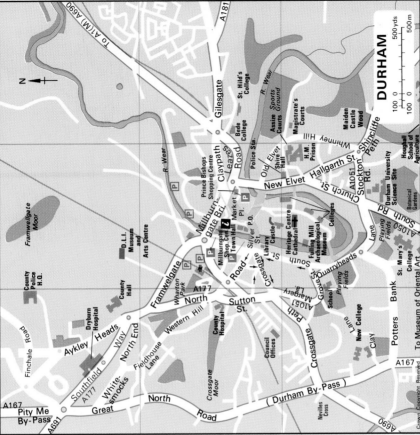

DURHAM

Aykley Heads	A1	New Elvet	B2
Church Street	C2	North End	A1
Clay Lane	C1	North Road	B1
Claypath	B2	Old Elvet	B2
Crossgate	A1	Pity Me By-Pass	A1
Crossgate Peth	C1	Potters Bank	C2
Durham By-Pass	B1	Quarryheads Lane	C2
Fieldhouse Lane	A1	Shincliffe Peth	C2
Finchale Road	A1	Silver Street	B2
Framwelgate	B1	South Road	C2
Gilesgate	B3	South Street	A2
Great North Road	A1	Southfield Way	A1
Grove Street	C1	Stockton Road	C2
Hallgarth Street	C2	Sutton Street	B1
Leazes Road	B2	Western Hill	B1
Margery Lane	C1	Whinney Hill	B2
Market Place	B2	Whitesmocks	A1
Millburngate Bridge	B2		

LOCAL RADIO

BBC RADIO NEWCASTLE 95.4 FM
SUN FM 103.4 FM, GALAXY 105-106 105.3/105.6/106.4 FM

TOURIST INFORMATION ☎ 0191 384 3720
MARKET PLACE, DURHAM,
COUNTY DURHAM, DH1 3NJ

HOSPITAL A & E ☎ 0191 333 2333
DRYBURN HOSPITAL, NORTH ROAD,
DURHAM, DH1 5TW

COUNCIL OFFICE ☎ 0191 386 4411
COUNTY HALL, DURHAM, DH1 5UB

EDINBURGH

STD Code 0131

EDINBURGH

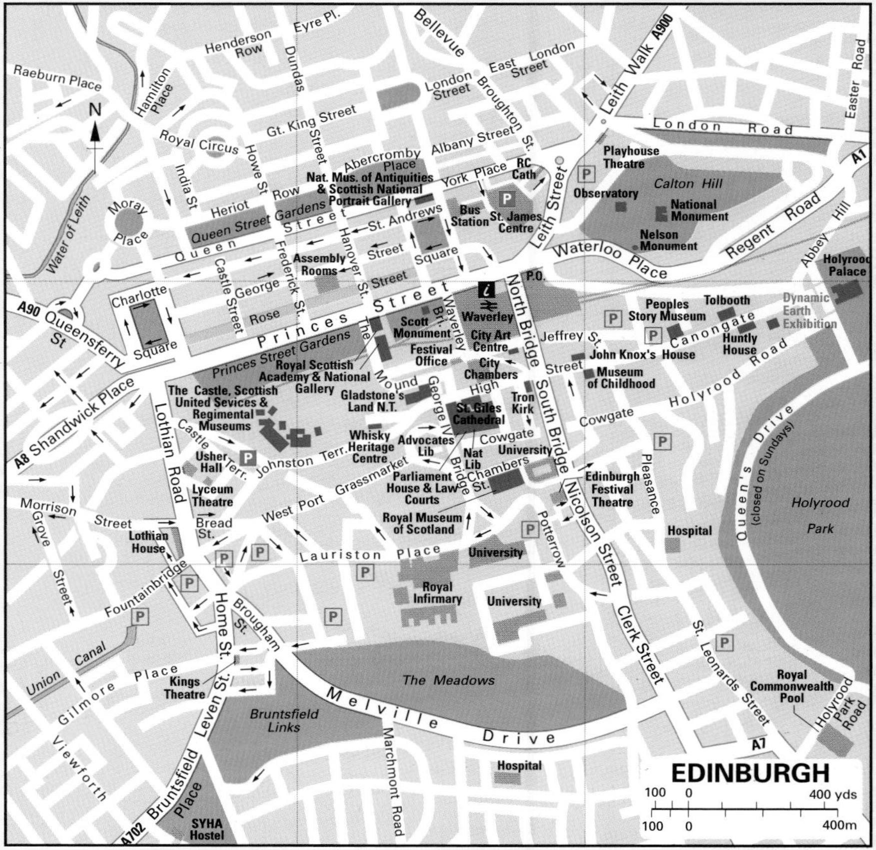

LOCAL RADIO

BBC RADIO SCOTLAND 810 AM & 92.4-94.7 FM
FORTH AM 1548 AM, FORTH FM 97.3 FM, SCOT FM 101.1 FM

TOURIST INFORMATION ☎ 0131 473 3800
INFORMATION CENTRE, 3 PRINCES STREET,
EDINBURGH, EH2 2QP

HOSPITAL A & E ☎ 0131 536 1000
ROYAL INFIRMARY OF EDINBURGH,
1 LAURISTON PLACE, EDINBURGH, EH3 9YW

COUNCIL OFFICE ☎ 0131 200 2000
CITY CHAMBERS, HIGH STREET,
EDINBURGH, EH1 1YJ

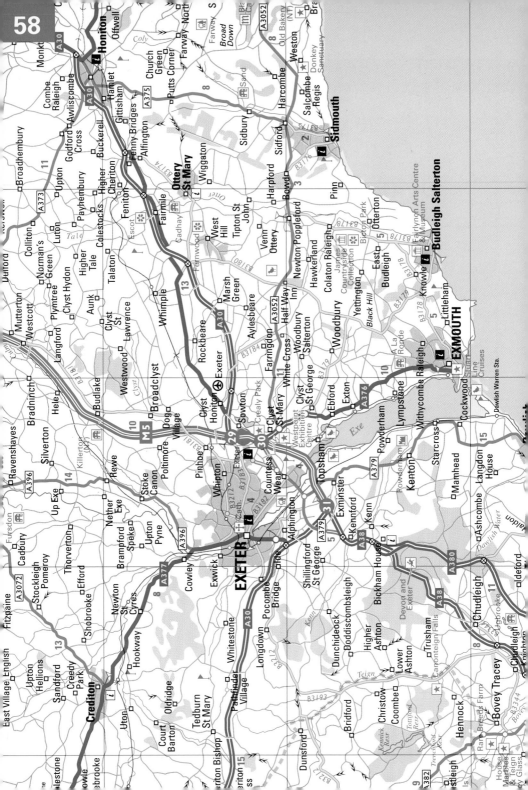

Crown Copyright Reserved

EXETER

400 yds
400m

Alphington Street	C1
Barnfield Road	B2
Bartholomew Street West	B1
Bedford Street	B2
Belmont Road	A3
Blackboy Road	A2
Blackall Road	A1
Bonhay Road	A1
Clifton Hill	A3
College Road	B3
Cowick Street	C1
Fore Street	B1
Heavitree Road	B3
Hele Road	A1
High Street	B2
Holloway Street	C2
Howell Road	A1
Longbrook Street	A2
Magdalen Road	B3
Magdalen Street	B2
Matford Lane	C3
Mount Pleasant Road	A3
New Bridge Street	C1
New North Road	A1/B2
Okehampton Road	C1
Okehampton Street	A3
Old Tiverton Road	A3
Paris Street	B2
Paul Street	B1
Pennsylvania Road	A2
Polsloe Road	A3
Prince of Wales Road	A1
Queen Street	B1
Richmond Road	B1
St. David's Hill	A1
Sidwell Street	B2
South Street	B2
The Quay	C2
Topsham Road	C2
Union Road	A2
Western Way	B3
Wonford Road	C3
York Road	A2

TOURIST INFORMATION ☎ 01392 265700
CIVIC CENTRE, PARIS STREET, EXETER
DEVON, EX1 1RP

HOSPITAL A & E ☎ 01392 411611
ROYAL DEVON & EXETER HOSPITAL (WONFORD),
BARRACK ROAD, EXETER, EX2 5DW

COUNCIL OFFICE ☎ 01392 277888
CIVIC CENTRE, PARIS STREET,
EXETER, EX1 1JN

LOCAL RADIO

BBC RADIO DEVON 95.8 FM
WESTWARD RADIO 666 AM, GEMINI FM 97 FM

DEAL

DOVER

FOLKESTONE

Hythe

ASHFORD

R o m n e y   M a r s h

FOLKESTONE Kent STD Code 01303

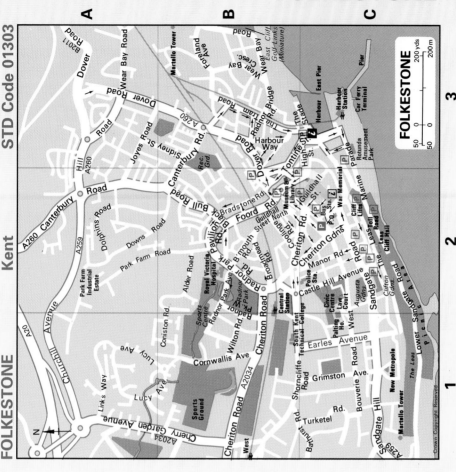

FOLKESTONE

200 yds
200 m
50   0   50

Alder Road	B2
Bathurst Road	C1
Black Bull Road	B2
Bournemouth Road	B2
Bouverie Road West	C1
Bradstone Road	B2
Broadmead Road	B2
Canterbury Road	A2/B3
Castle Hill Avenue	C2
Cheriton Gardens	C2
Cheriton Road	B1
Cherry Garden Avenue	B1
Churchill Avenue	A1
Coniston Road	B2
Coolinge Road	B1
Cornwallis Avenue	B2
Dolphins Road	A2
Dover Road	A2
Downs Road	A2
Earles Avenue	C1
Foord Road	B2
Foreland Avenue	B3
Grimston Avenue	C1
Guildhall Street	C2
Guildhall Street North	B2
Harbour Way	B3

High Street	C3
Hill Road	A3
Joyes Road	A3
Links Way	A1
Lower Sandgate Road	C2
Lucy Avenue	A1
Manor Road	C2
Marine Parade	C2
Park Farm Road	A2
Pavilion Road	B2
Radnor Bridge Road	B3
Radnor Park Avenue	B1
Radnor Park Road	B2
Radnor Park West	B1
Sandgate Hill	C1
Sandgate Road	C2
Shorncliffe Road	B1
Sidney Street	B3
The Leas	C2
The Stade	B3
The Tram Road	B3
Tontine Street	C1
Turketel Road	B1
Wear Bay Crescent	A3
Wear Bay Road	A3
Wilton Road	B1

LOCAL RADIO

BBC RADIO KENT 97.6 FM
CHANNEL TRAVEL RADIO 107.6 FM, INVICTA FM 97 FM

TOURIST INFORMATION ☎ 01303 258594
HARBOUR STREET, FOLKESTONE,
KENT, CT20 1QN

HOSPITAL A & E ☎ 01233 633331
WILLIAM HARVEY HOSPITAL, KENNINGTON RD,
WILLESBOROUGH, ASHFORD, TN24 OLZ

COUNCIL OFFICE ☎ 01303 850388
CIVIC CENTRE, CASTLE HILL AVENUE,
FOLKESTONE, CT20 2QY

Crown Copyright Reserved

STD Code 0141

GLASGOW

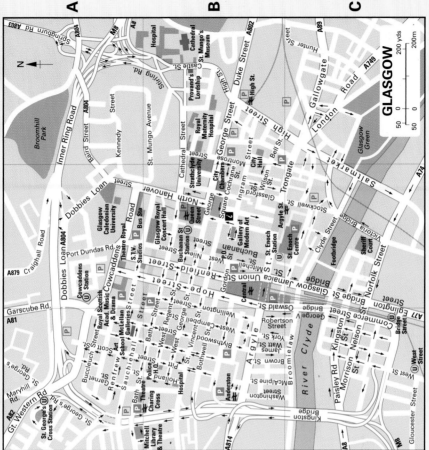

GLASGOW

0   50
0   50

0   200 yds
0   200m

LOCAL RADIO

BBC RADIO SCOTLAND 810 AM & 92.4-94.7 FM
CLYDE 2 1152 AM, CLYDE 1 102.5 FM, SCOT FM 100.3 FM

TOURIST INFORMATION ☎ 0141 204 4400
11 GEORGE SQUARE, GLASGOW, G2 1DY

HOSPITAL A & E ☎ 0141 211 2000
WESTERN INFIRMARY, DUMBARTON ROAD,
GLASGOW, G11 6NT

COUNCIL OFFICE ☎ 0141 287 2000
CITY CHAMBERS, GEORGE SQUARE,
GLASGOW, G2 1DU

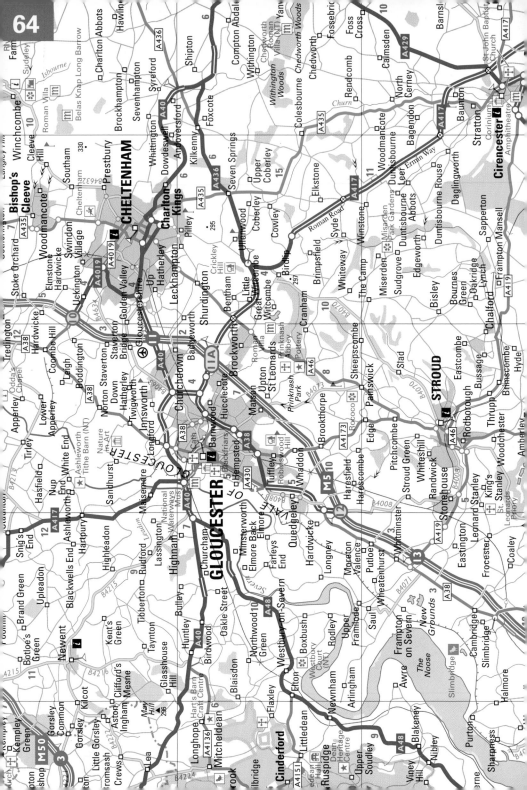

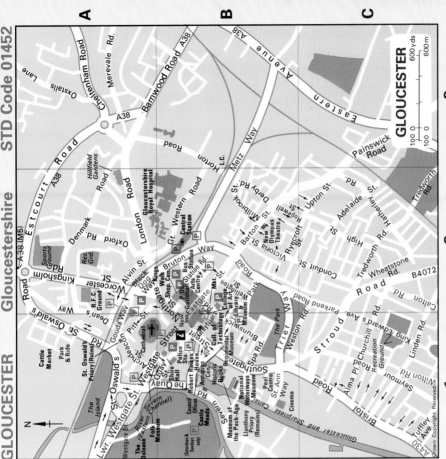

GLOUCESTER

100	0		
100	0	600m	
	600yds		

Crown Copyright Reserved

TOURIST INFORMATION ☎ 01452 421188
28 SOUTHGATE STREET, GLOUCESTER,
GLOUCESTERSHIRE, GL1 2DP

HOSPITAL A & E ☎ 01452 528555
GLOUCESTER ROYAL HOSPITAL
GREAT WESTERN RD, GLOUCESTER, GL1 3NN

COUNCIL OFFICE ☎ 01452 522232
COUNCIL OFFICES, NORTH WAREHOUSE,
THE DOCKS, GLOUCESTER, GL1 2EP

LOCAL RADIO

BBC RADIO GLOUCESTERSHIRE 104.7 FM
CLASSIC GOLD 774 AM, SEVERN SOUND FM 102.4 FM

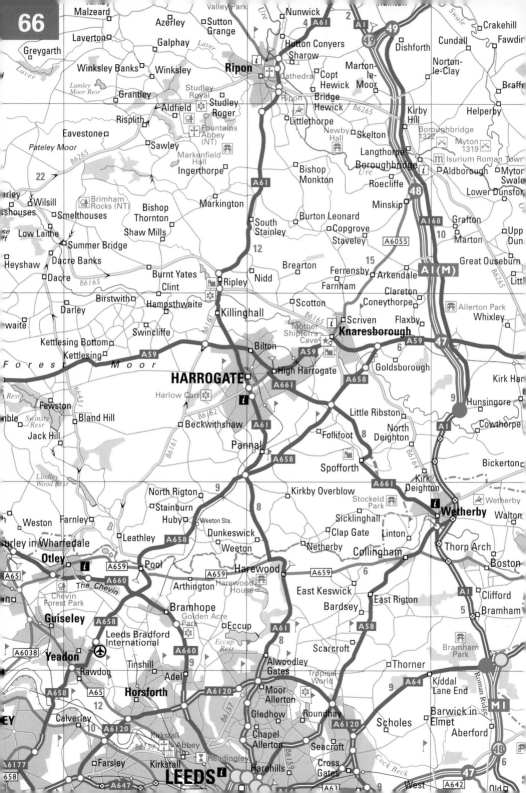

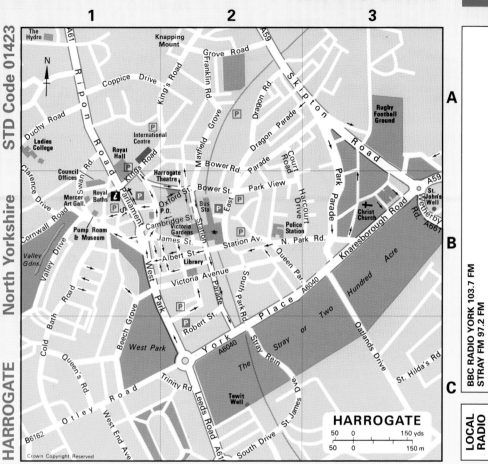

Albert Street	B2	East Parade	B2	Park Parade	B3	Station Parade	B2
Beech Grove	C1	Franklin Road	A2	Park View	B2	Stray Rein	C2
Bower Road	A2	Grove Road	A2	Parliament Street	B1	Swan Road	B1
Bower Street	B2	Harcourt Drive	B3	Queen Parade	B2	Trinity Road	C2
Cambridge Street	B1	James Street	B2	Queen's Road	C1	Valley Drive	B1
Clarence Drive	B1	King's Road	B1	Ripon Road	A1	Victoria Avenue	B2
Cold Bath Road	C1	Knaresborough Road	B3	Robert Street	C2	West End Avenue	C1
Coppice Drive	A1	Leeds Road	C2	St. Hilda's Road	C3	West Park	B1
Cornwall Road	B1	Mayfield Grove	A2	St. James Drive	C2	Wetherby Road	B3
Court Road	A2	North Park Road	B2	Skipton Road	A2	York Place	C2
Dragon Parade	A2	Oatlands Drive	C3	South Drive	C2		
Dragon Road	A2	Otley Road	C1	South Park Road	B2		
Duchy Road	A1	Oxford Street	B2	Station Avenue	B2		

TOURIST INFORMATION ☎ 01423 537300
ROYAL BATHS ASSEMBLY ROOMS, CRES. ROAD,
HARROGATE, NORTH YORKSHIRE, HG1 2RR

HOSPITAL A & E ☎ 01423 885959
HARROGATE DISTRICT HOSPITAL,
LANCASTER PARK ROAD, HARROGATE, HG2 7SX

COUNCIL OFFICE ☎ 01423 568954
COUNCIL OFFICES, CRESCENT GARDENS
HARROGATE, HG1 2SG

Kimbolton
A4112
Grafton
Wolferlow
Eyton
Stockton
Whyle
Collington
High Lane
Cobnash
A4361
Bach Camp
Hatfield
Thornbury
Edvin
Shirl Heath
Lawton
Cholstrey
Leominster
Pudleston
Wall Hills
Loach
B4529
Arrow
Steen's Bridge
Grendon Green
Edwyn Ralph
Burton Court
Stretford Court
Monkland
A44
Stoke Prior
11
Docklow
A44
Bredenbury
Bromyard
Sollers
Dilwyn
Ivington
Ivington Green
Humber Court
Bromyard Downs
Brock
10
Brierley
Wharton
Risbury
Marston Stannett
Dilwyn Common
Aulden
A49
B4361
Little Cowarne
Munderfield Row
Stanf
Bish
15
Birley
Upper Hill
Hope under Dinmore
Bowley
11
Pencombe
Munderfield Stocks
Acton Beauch
Knapton Green
A4112
A4110
Bodenham
Maund Bryan
Ullingswick
A465
Stoke Lacy
Bishop's Frome
Weobley Marsh
Bush Bank
King's Pyon
Westhope
Queenswood
Bodenham Moor
A417
Five Bridges
gemoor
Dinmore Manor
13
Urdimarsh
The Vauld
Felton
Moreton Jeffries
Castle Frome
Canon Pyon
Walker's Green
Preston Wynne
Burley Gate
Much Cowarne
Wormsley
Wellington
Marden
Ocle Pychard
2
Newtown
Lower Egleton
Canon Frome
12
Yarsop
Foxley
Tillington Common
Wellington Marsh
Sutton Walls
7
Westhide
Stretton Grandison
Yazor
A480
Mansell Lacy
Tillington
Moreton on Lugg
Sutton St Nicholas
Withington
8
Yarkhill
Ashperton
nsell
nage
Brinsop
Burghill
Pipe and Lyde
Shelwick
A465
Shucknall
A4103
Bishopstone
Credenhill
Stretton Sugwas
Holmer
Hagley
Weston Beggard
A438
Tarrington
4
A438
13
Kenchester
A4103
Hereford
Logwardine
Bartestree
A417
Trumpet
Wall Gree
Bridge Sollers
The Weir (NT)
Swainshill
HEREFORD
Tupsley
Dormington
Prior's Frome
Canon Bridge
Upper Breinton
White Cross
Cath
Rotherwas Chapel
Checkley
Aylton
3
Lulham
Breinton
A465
Lower Bullingham
Hampton Bishop
Putley
A4172
Madley
Eaton Bishop
Belmont Abbey
Grafton
Dinedor
Holme Lacy
Mordiford
Little Marcle
ore
Clehonger
A4349
A49
Fiddler's Green
Woolhope
A449
Webton
Kingstone
Allensmore
Twyford Common
Fownhope
Sollers Hope
Rushall
Much Marcle
Thruxton
Callow
Dewsall Court
Aconbury
Bolstone
Brockhampton
Tillers
Whitfield
11
Didley
Kingsthorne
Little Birch
Little Dewchurch
Ballingham
Carey
How Caple Court
Yatton Wood
8
ormbridge
Kilpeck
Much Dewchurch
Much Birch
Penalt
Fawley Chapel
How Caple
St Mary's Church
Kem
Howton
Wormelow Tump
Hoarwithy
Foy
Hole-in-the-Wall
Upton Bishop
M50
Kenderchurch
Orcop Hill
Llandinabo
Kings Caple
Baysham
Brampton Abbotts
Crow Hill
3
ontrilas
Bagwyllydiart
A466
Harewood End
Sellack
angua
Kentchurch
Garway Hill
Pencoyd
Michaelchurch
A49
Bridstow
Ross Spur
Rudhall
Linton
Gorsle
366
Sandyway
St Owen's Cross
5
Ross-on-Wye
Bromsash
Aston Crews
Little Garway
17
St Weonards
Tretire
Peterstow
Hom Green
Weston under Penyard
Garway
A4137
Glewstone
A40
Pontshill
Lea
Graig
Skenfrith (NT)
Llangarron
Pencraig
Hillcourt
9
Broad Oak
11
Goodrich
Coughton

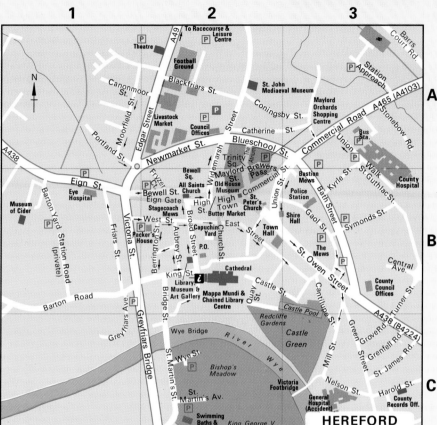

STD Code 01432

Herefordshire

HEREFORD

BBC RADIO HEREFORD & WORCESTER 104 FM
WYVERN FM 96.7 FM

LOCAL RADIO

Aubrey Street	B2	Catherine Street	A2	Greyfriars Bridge	C2	St. James Road	C3
Barrs Court Road	A3	Central Avenue	B3	Grove Road	C3	St. Martin's Avenue	C2
Barton Road	B1	Church Street	B2	Harold Street	C3	St. Martin's Street	C2
Barton Yard	B1	Commercial Road	A3	High Street	B2	St. Owen Street	B3
Bath Street	B3	Commercial Street	B2	High Town	B2	Station Approach	A3
Berrington Street	B2	Coningsby Street	A2	King Street	B2	Station Road	B1
Bewell Street	B2	East Street	B2	Kyrle Street	B3	Stonebow Road	A3
Blackfriars Street	A2	Edgar Street	A2	Maylord Street	B2	Symonds Street	B3
Blueschool Street	A2	Eign Gate	B2	Mill Street	C3	Turner Street	B3
Bridge Street	B2	Eign Street	B1	Moorfield Street	A1	Union Street	B2
Broad Street	B2	Friars Street	B1	Nelson Street	C3	Union Walk	A3
Canonmoor Street	A1	Gaol Street	B3	Newmarket Street	A2	Victoria Street	B1
Cantilupe Street	B3	Green Street	C3	Portland Street	A1	West Street	B2
Capuchin Court	B2	Grenfell Road	C3	Quay Street	B2	Widemarsh Street	A2
Castle Street	B2	Greyfriars Avenue	C1	St. Guthiac Street	B3	Wye Street	C2

TOURIST INFORMATION ☎ 01432 268430
1 KING STREET, HEREFORD, HR4 9BW

HOSPITAL A & E ☎ 01432 355444
HEREFORD GENERAL HOSPITAL,
NELSON STREET, HEREFORD, HR1 2PA

COUNCIL OFFICE ☎ 01432 364500
COUNCIL OFFICES, ST. OWEN STREET,
HEREFORD, HR1 2PJ

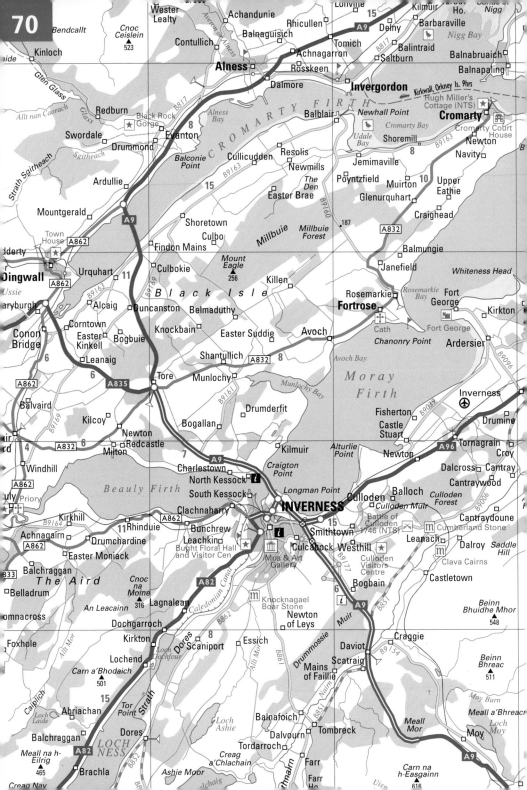

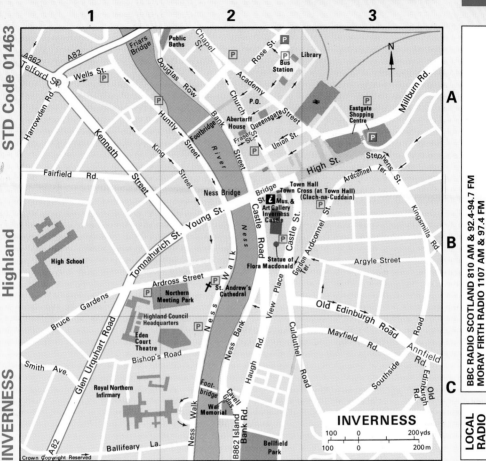

BBC RADIO SCOTLAND 810 AM & 92.4-94.7 FM
MORAY FIRTH RADIO 1107 AM & 97.4 FM

LOCAL RADIO

Academy Street	A2	Castle Street	B2	High Street	A3	Rose Street	A2
Annfield Road	C3	Cavell Gardens	C2	Huntly Street	A2	Smith Avenue	C1
Ardconnel Street	B3	Chapel Street	A2	Island Bank Road	C2	Southside Road	C3
Ardconnel Terrace	B3	Church Street	A2	Kenneth Street	A1	Stephens Street	A3
Ardross Street	B1	Culduthel Road	C2	King Street	A1	Telford Street	A1
Argyle Street	B3	Douglas Row	A2	Kingsmills Road	B3	Tomnahurich Street	B1
Ballifeary Lane	C1	Fairfield Road	B1	Mayfield Road	C3	Union Street	A2
Bank Street	A2	Fraser Street	A2	Millburn Road	A3	View Place	B2
Bishop's Road	C1	Glen Urquhart Road	C1	Ness Bank	C2	Wells Street	A1
Bridge Street	B2	Gordon Terrace	B2	Ness Walk	C2	Young Street	B2
Bruce Gardens	C1	Harrowden Road	A1	Old Edinburgh Road	B3		
Castle Road	B2	Haugh Road	C2	Queensgate	A2		

TOURIST INFORMATION ☎ 01463 234353
CASTLE WYND, INVERNESS, HIGHLAND, IV2 3BJ

HOSPITAL A & E ☎ 01463 704000
RAIGMORE HOSPITAL, OLD PERTH ROAD,
INVERNESS, IV2 3UJ

COUNCIL OFFICE ☎ 01463 702000
COUNCIL OFFICES, GLENURQUHART ROAD,
INVERNESS, IV3 5NX

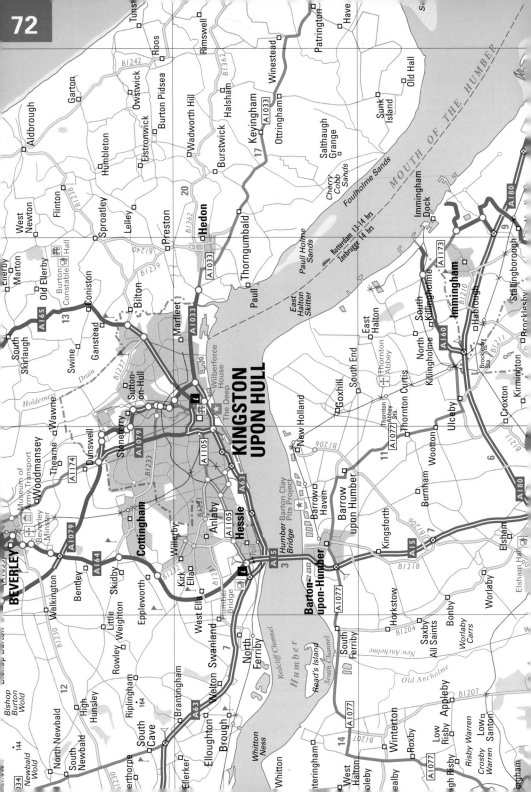

STD Code 01482

KINGSTON UPON HULL

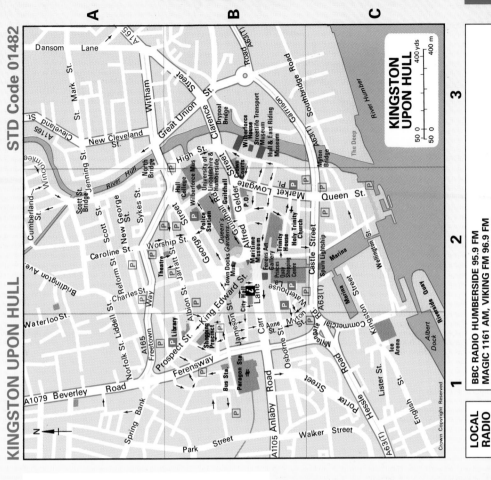

KINGSTON UPON HULL

50 0   400 yds
50 0   400 m

Crown Copyright Reserved

LOCAL RADIO

BBC RADIO HUMBERSIDE 95.9 FM
MAGIC 1161 AM, VIKING FM 96.9 FM

TOURIST INFORMATION ☎ 01482 223559
1 PARAGON STREET,
KINGSTON UPON HULL, HU1 3NA

HOSPITAL A & E ☎ 01482 328541
HULL ROYAL INFIRMARY, ANLABY ROAD,
KINGSTON UPON HULL, HU3 2JZ

COUNCIL OFFICE ☎ 01482 610610
GUILDHALL, ALFRED GELDER STREET,
KINGSTON UPON HULL, HU1 2AA

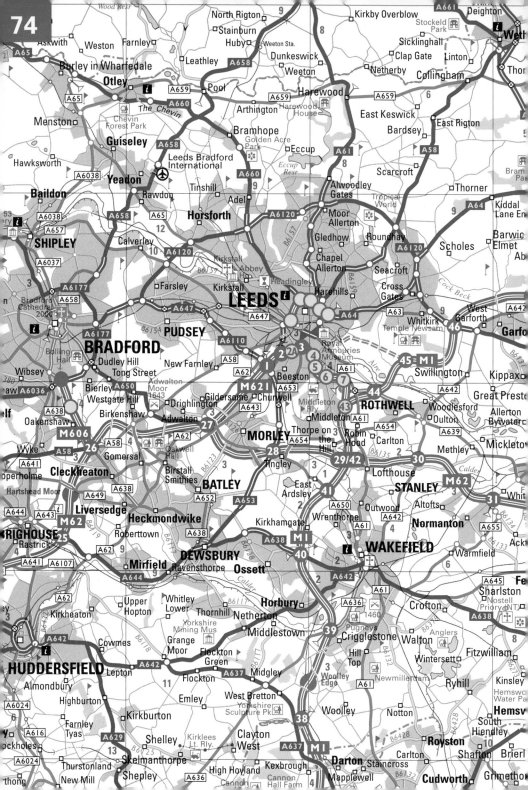

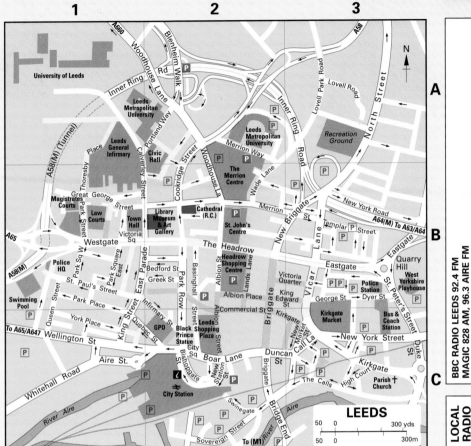

LEEDS

STD Code 0113

West Yorkshire

LEEDS

Aire Street	C1	Dyer Street	B3	New Briggate	B2	St. Peter's Street	B3
Albion Place	B2	East Parade	B1	New Market Street	C3	Swinegate	C2
Albion Street	B2	Eastgate	B3	New Station Street	C2	Templar Street	B3
Basinghall Street	B2	George Street	B3	New York Road	B3	The Calls	C3
Bedford Street	B2	Great George Street	B1	New York Street	C3	The Headrow	B2
Blenheim Walk	A2	Greek Street	B2	North Street	A3	Thoresby Place	B1
Boar Lane	C2	High Court	C3	Park Place	B1	Vicar Lane	B3
Bridge End	C2	Infirmary Street	B1	Park Row	B2	Victoria Quarter	B2
Briggate	C2	Inner Ring Road	A1	Park Square East	B1	Victoria Square	B1
Call Lane	C3	King Edward Street	B2	Park Square West	B1	Wade Lane	B2
Calverley Street	A1	King Street	C1	Park Street	B1	Wellington Street	C1
City Square	C2	Kirkgate	C3	Portland Way	A2	Westgate	B1
Commercial Street	B2	Lands Lane	B2	Quebec Street	C1	Whitehall Road	C1
Cookridge Street	B2	Lovell Park Road	A3	Queen Street	C1	Woodhouse Lane	A1
Duke Street	C3	Lovell Road	A3	Somers Street	B1	York Place	C1
Duncan Street	C2	Merrion Centre	B2	Sovereign Street	C2		
		Merrion Way	A2	St. Paul's Street	B1		

TOURIST INFORMATION ☎ 0113 242 5242
GATEWAY YORKSHIRE, THE ARCADE,
CITY STATION, LEEDS, W. YORKSHIRE, LS1 1PL

HOSPITAL A & E ☎ 0113 243 2799
LEEDS GENERAL INFIRMARY,
GREAT GEORGE STREET, LEEDS, LS1 3EX

COUNCIL OFFICE ☎ 0113 247 4023
CIVIC HALL, CALVERLEY STREET,
LEEDS, LS1 1UR

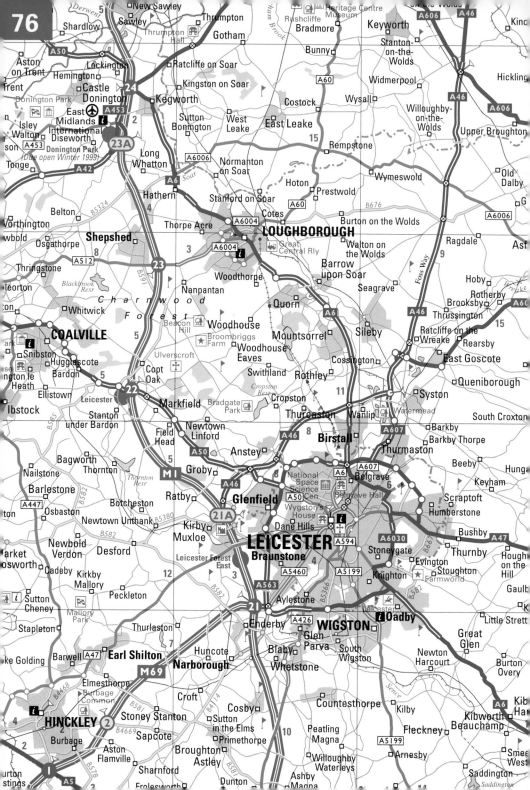

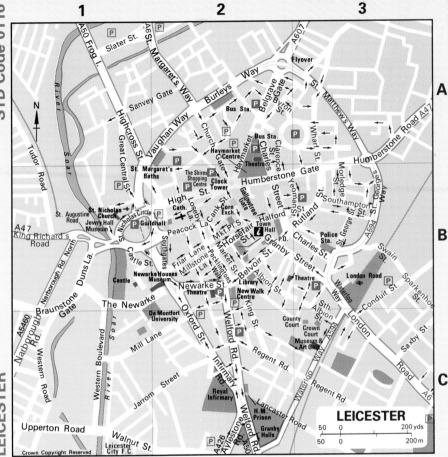

LEICESTER

LEICESTER

Crown Copyright Reserved

Albion Street	B2	Granby Street	B2	Market Street	B2	Saxby Street	C3
Aylestone Road	C2	Great Central Street	A1	Mill Lane	C1	Slater Street	A1
Belgrave Gate	A2	Halford Street	B2	Millstone Lane	B2	South Albion Street	B3
Belvoir Street	B2	Haymarket	B2	Morledge Street	B3	Southampton Street	B3
Braunstone Gate	B1	High Street	B2	Narborough Road	C1	Southgates	B2
Burleys Way	A2	Highcross Street	A1	Narborough Road	B1	Sparkenhoe Street	B3
Byron Street	A2	Horsfair Street	B2	North		Swain Street	B3
Cank Street	B2	Humberstone Gate	B2	Newarke Street	B2	The Newarke	B1
Castle Street	B1	Humberstone Road	A3	Oxford Street	B2	Tudor Road	A1
Charles Street	A2	Infirmary Road	C2	Peacock Lane	B2	Upperton Road	C1
Church Gate	A2	Jarrom Street	C1	Pocklingtons Walk	B2	Vaughan Way	A2
Clarence Street	A2	King Richard's Road	B1	Regent Road	C2	Walnut Street	C1
Conduit Street	B3	King Street	B2	Rutland Street	B3	Waterloo Way	C3
Duns Lane	B1	Lancaster Road	C2	St. George Street	B3	Welford Road	C2
Friar Lane	B2	London Road	C3	St. George's Way	B3	Western Boulevard	C1
Frog Island	A1	Loseby Lane	B2	St. Margaret's Way	A1	Western Road	C1
Gallowtree Gate	B2	Market Place South	B2	St. Matthew's Way	A3	Wharf Street	A3
				St. Nicholas Circle	B1	Yeoman Street	B2
				Sanvey Gare	A1		

TOURIST INFORMATION ☎ 0116 299 8888
7 - 9 EVERY STREET, TOWN HALL SQUARE,
LEICESTER, LE1 6AG

HOSPITAL A & E ☎ 0116 254 1414
LEICESTER ROYAL INFIRMARY,
INFIRMARY SQUARE, LEICESTER, LE1 5WW

COUNCIL OFFICE ☎ 0116 254 9922
COUNCIL OFFICES, NEW WALK CENTRE,
WELFORD PLACE, LEICESTER, LE1 6ZG

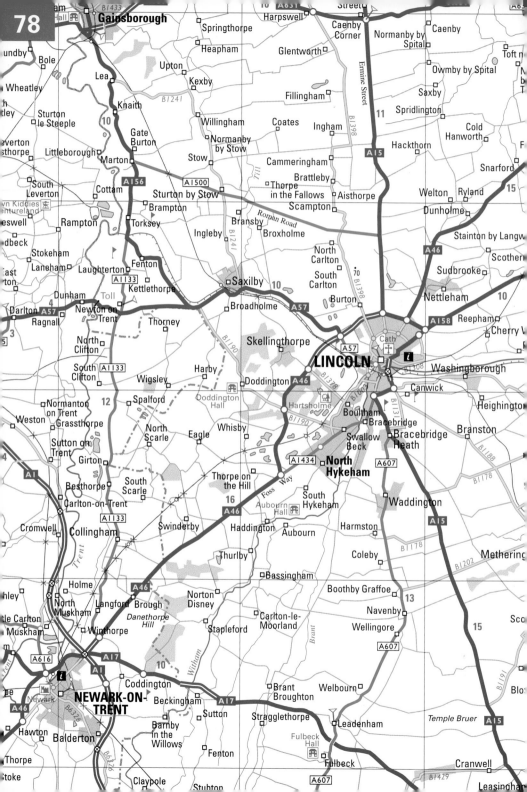

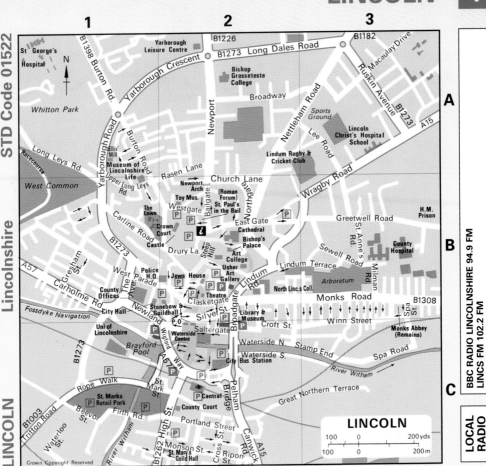

STD Code 01522

Lincolnshire

LINCOLN

BBC RADIO LINCOLNSHIRE 94.9 FM
LINCS FM 102.2 FM

LOCAL RADIO

TOURIST INFORMATION ☎ 01522 873700
9 CASTLE HILL, LINCOLN,
LINCOLNSHIRE, LN1 3AA

HOSPITAL A & E ☎ 01522 512512
LINCOLN COUNTY HOSPITAL,
GREETWELL ROAD, LINCOLN, LN2 5QY

COUNCIL OFFICE ☎ 01522 881188
CITY HALL, BEAUMONT FEE,
LINCOLN, LN1 1DD

LIVERPOOL Merseyside STD Code 0151

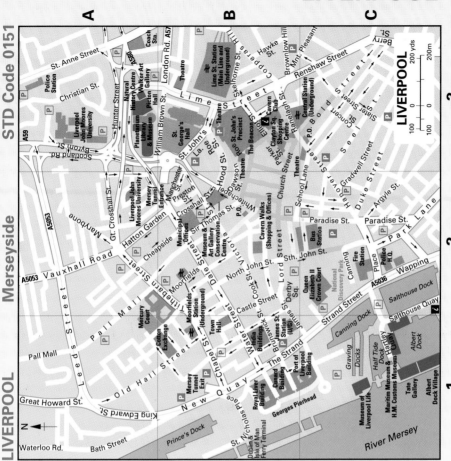

LOCAL RADIO

BBC RADIO MERSEYSIDE 95.8 FM
MAGIC 1548 AM, RADIO CITY 96.7 FM, CRASH FM 107.6 FM

TOURIST INFORMATION ☎ 0151 709 3631
MERSEYSIDE WELCOME CENTRE, CLAYTON SQ.
SHOPPING CEN, LIVERPOOL, MERSEYSIDE, L1 1QR

HOSPITAL A & E ☎ 0151 525 5980
UNIVERSITY HOSPITAL OF AINTREE, LOWER
LANE, FAZAKERLEY, LIVERPOOL, L9 7AL

COUNCIL OFFICE ☎ 0151 227 3911
MUNICIPAL BUILDINGS, DALE STREET,
LIVERPOOL, L69 2DH

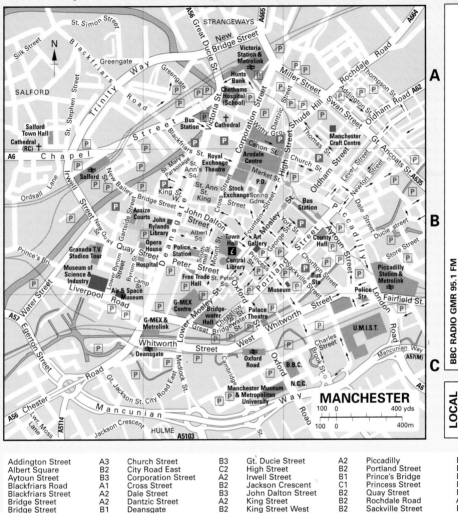

STD Code 0161

Greater Manchester

MANCHESTER

BBC RADIO GMR 95.1 FM
MAGIC 1152 MANCHESTER 1152 AM, 1458 LIGHT AM, 1458 AM, GALAXY 102 FM, KEY 103 FM

LOCAL RADIO

TOURIST INFORMATION ☎ 0161 234 3157/8
MANCHESTER VISITOR CENTRE, TOWN HALL
EXTENSION, LLOYD ST, MANCHESTER, M60 2LA

HOSPITAL A & E ☎ 0161 276 1234
MANCHESTER ROYAL INFIRMARY,
OXFORD ROAD, MANCHESTER, M13 9WL

COUNCIL OFFICE ☎ 0161 234 5600
TOWN HALL, ALBERT SQUARE,
MANCHESTER, M60 2LA

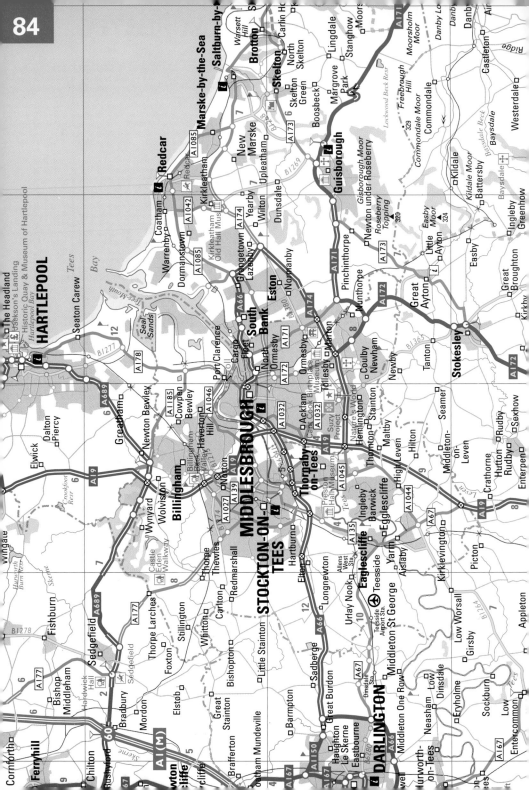

STD Code 01642

MIDDLESBROUGH

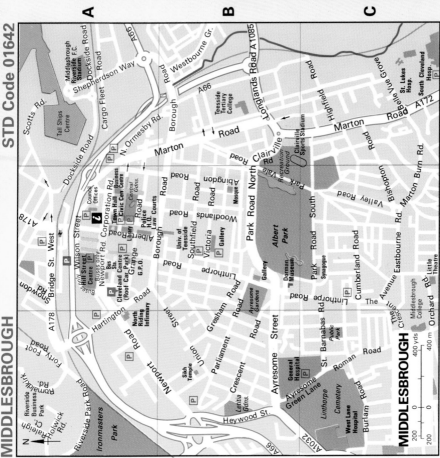

TOURIST INFORMATION ☎ 01642 264330/243425
51 CORPORATION ROAD,
MIDDLESBROUGH, TS1 1LT

HOSPITAL A & E ☎ 01642 617617
NORTH TEES GENERAL HOSPITAL, HARDWICK
ROAD, STOCKTON-ON-TEES, TS19 8PE

COUNCIL OFFICE ☎ 01642 245432
MUNICIPAL BUILDINGS, PO BOX 99A,
RUSSELL STREET, MIDDLESBROUGH, TS1 2QQ

LOCAL RADIO

BBC RADIO CLEVELAND 95 FM
MAGIC 1170 AM, TFM 96.6 FM, CENTURY RADIO 100.7 FM

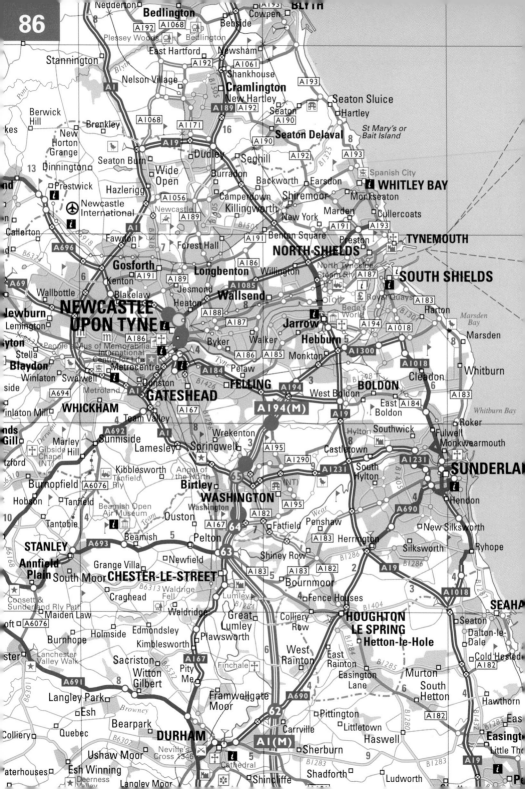

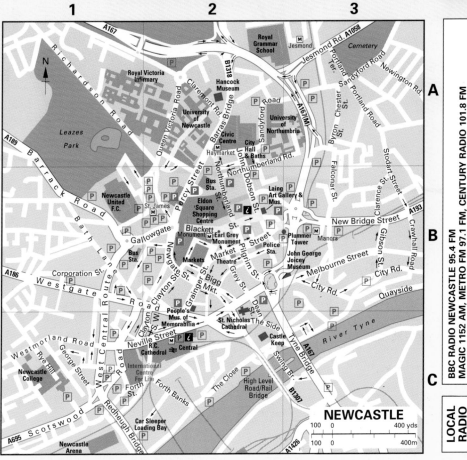

STD Code 0191

Tyne & Wear

NEWCASTLE

BBC RADIO NEWCASTLE 95.4 FM
MAGIC 1152 AM, METRO FM 97.1 FM, CENTURY RADIO 101.8 FM

LOCAL RADIO

Barrack Road	A1	Crawhall Road	B3	Melbourne Street	B3	Richardson Road	A1
Barras Bridge	A2	Dean Street	B2	Neville Street	C1	Rye Hill	C1
Bath Lane	B1	Falconar Street	A3	New Bridge Street	B3	Sandyford Road	A2
Bigg Market	B2	Forth Banks	C2	Newgate Street	B2	Scotswood Road	C1
Blackett Street	B2	Forth Street	C1	Newington Road	A3	Stodart Street	A3
Byron Street	A3	Gallowgate	B1	Northumberland Road	B2	Swing Bridge	C2
Chester Street	A3	George Street	C1	Percy Street	B2	The Close	C2
City Road	B3	Gibson Street	B3	Pilgrim Street	B2	The Side	B2
Claremont Road	A2	Grainger Street	B2	Portland Road	A3	Tyne Bridge	C3
Clarence Street	B3	Grey Street	B2	Portland Terrace	A3	West Central Route	C1
Clayton Street	B2	Jesmond Road	A3	Quayside	B3	Westgate Road	B1
Clayton Street West	C1	John Dobson Street	A2	Queen Victoria Road	A2	Westmorland Road	C1
Corporation Street	B1	Market Street	B2	Redheugh Bridge	C1		

TOURIST INFORMATION ☎ **0191 261 0610**
CENTRAL LIBRARY, PRINCESS SQ, NEWCASTLE
UPON TYNE, TYNE & WEAR, NE99 1DX

HOSPITAL A & E ☎ **0191 232 5131**
ROYAL VICTORIA INFIRMARY, QUEEN VICTORIA
ROAD, NEWCASTLE UPON TYNE, NE1 4LP

COUNCIL OFFICE ☎ **0191 232 8520**
CIVIC CENTRE, BARRAS BRIDGE,
NEWCASTLE UPON TYNE, NE99 2BN

NORFOLK

BROADS

NORWICH

Bastwick
Rollesby
Thrigby Hall
Wickhampton
Halvergate
Wickham
Lower Thurlton
Thorpe
Maypole Green
Toft

B1152
Repps
Clippesby
Burgh St Margaret
Billockby
Stokesby
Damgate
Tunstall
Moulton St Mary
Freethorpe
Freethorpe Common
Pettitts Animal Adventure Park
Norton Subcourse
Ravningham
A143

Clear Water 2000
Catfield
Ludham
Upper Street
St Helen
Ranworth
South Walsham
Upton
Upton Green
Acle
North Burlingham
Lingwood
Beighton
Strumpshaw
South Burlingham
Southwood
Limpenhoe
Hales
HeckIngham
Hales Hall
Kirby Cane
A146

Beeston St Lawrence
Turf
Neatishead
Irstead
Woodbastwick
Salhouse
Hemblington
Blofield
Brundall
Buckenham
Cantley
Hassingham
Langley Street
Chedgrave
Loddon
Mundham
The Laurels
Thwaite

Hoveton
Horning
Rackheath
New Rackheath
Thorpe End Garden Village
Thorpe St Andrew
Little Plumstead
Great Plumstead
Postwick
Surlingham
Rockland St Mary
Hellington
Thurton
Bergh Apton
Sisland
Seething
Kirstead Green
Woodton

Wroxham
Belaugh
Crostwick
Sprowston
Trowse Newton
Kirby Bedon
Bramerton
Framingham Pigot
Framingham Earl
Yelverton
Poringland
Alpington
Brooke
Howe
Shotesham
Woottn

Rackheath
New Rackheath
Catton
Spixworth
Castle
Mus
Lakenham
Caistor St Edmund
Dunston
Stoke Holy Cross
Swainsthorpe
Saxlingham Nethergate
Saxlingham Thorpe
Hempnall

Sco Ruston
Coltishall
Horstead
Hainford
Frettenham
Newton St Faith
Horsham St Faith
Norwich
Eaton
Keswick
Swardeston
Mulbarton
Newton Flotman
Hapton
Forncett St Mary
Tasburgh
Tharston

Buxton
Stratton Strawless
Waterloo
Horsford
Hellesdon
New Costessey
Bowthorpe
Earlham
Colney
Cringleford
Intwood
East Carleton
Bracon Ash
Rainthorpe Hall
Flordon
Tacolneston

Hevingham
St Helena
Drayton
Costessey
Taverham
Easton
Marlingford
Bawburgh
Little Melton
Hethersett
Ketteringham
Wreningham
Ashwellthorpe
Fundenhall
Bunwell Street

Buxton Heath
Felthorpe
Attlebridge
Ringland
Weston Longville
Weston Green
Colton
Honingham
Barford
Great Melton
Wramplingham
High Green
Wymondham
Silfield
Hapton

Booton
Whitwell
Brandiston
Alderford
Morton
Mattishall Burgh
East Tuddenham
South Green
Welborne
Barnham Broom
Coston
Kimberley
Crownthorpe
Wicklewood
Morley St Botolph
Suton
Deopham
Spooner Row
Besthorpe
Attleborough

Bawdeswell
Sparham
Lyng
Lenwade
Primrose Green
North Tuddenham
Hockering
Mattishall
Runhall
Thuxton
Hackford
Hingham
Deopham Green

A1067
A149
A1062
A1151
A1150
A140
A1042
A1074
A47
A11
A1067
A140
A146
A143
A1064
A1152
B1149
B1354
B1108
B1113
B1135
B1172
B1136
B1332
B1140

STD Code 01603 · Norfolk · NORWICH

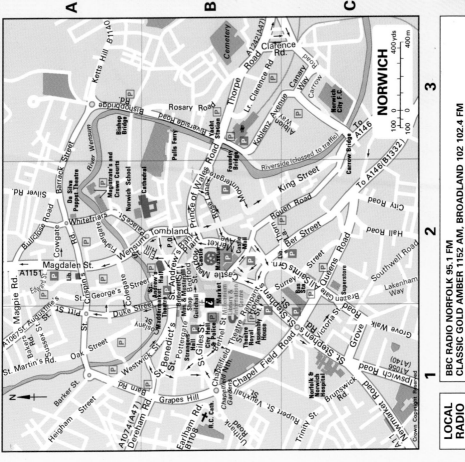

LOCAL RADIO

BBC RADIO NORFOLK 95.1 FM
CLASSIC GOLD AMBER 1152 AM, BROADLAND 102 102.4 FM

TOURIST INFORMATION ☎ 01603 666071
THE GUILDHALL, GAOL HILL, NORWICH,
NORFOLK, NR2 1NF

HOSPITAL A & E ☎ 01603 286286
NORFOLK & NORWICH HOSPITAL,
BRUNSWICK ROAD, NORWICH, NR1 3SR

COUNCIL OFFICE ☎ 01603 622233
CITY HALL, ST. PETER'S STREET,
NORWICH, NR2 1NH

STD Code 0115

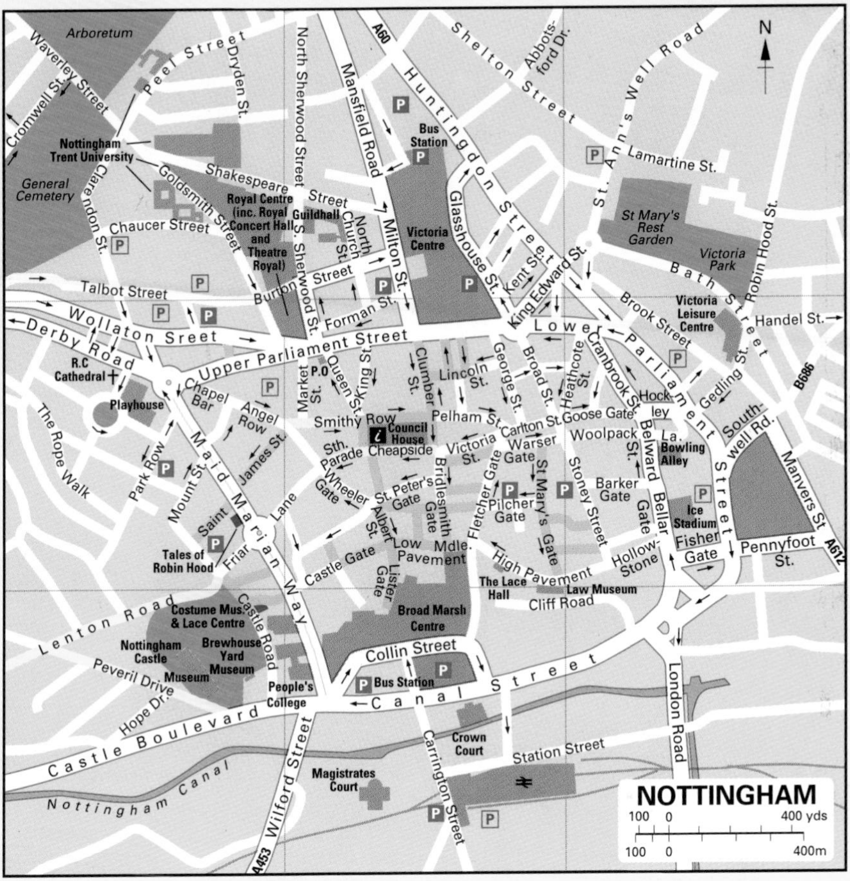

NOTTINGHAM

BBC RADIO NOTTINGHAM 95.5 FM
CLASSIC GOLD GEM 999 AM, TRENT FM 96.2 FM

LOCAL RADIO

NOTTINGHAM

100 0 400 yds
100 0 400m

TOURIST INFORMATION ☎ 0115 915 5330
1-4 SMITHY ROW, NOTTINGHAM, NG1 2BY

HOSPITAL A & E ☎ 0115 924 9924
QUEENS MEDICAL CENTRE, UNIVERSITY HOSP,
DERBY ROAD, NOTTINGHAM, NG7 2UH

COUNCIL OFFICE ☎ 0115 915 5555
THE GUILDHALL, BURTON STREET,
NOTTINGHAM, NG1 4BT

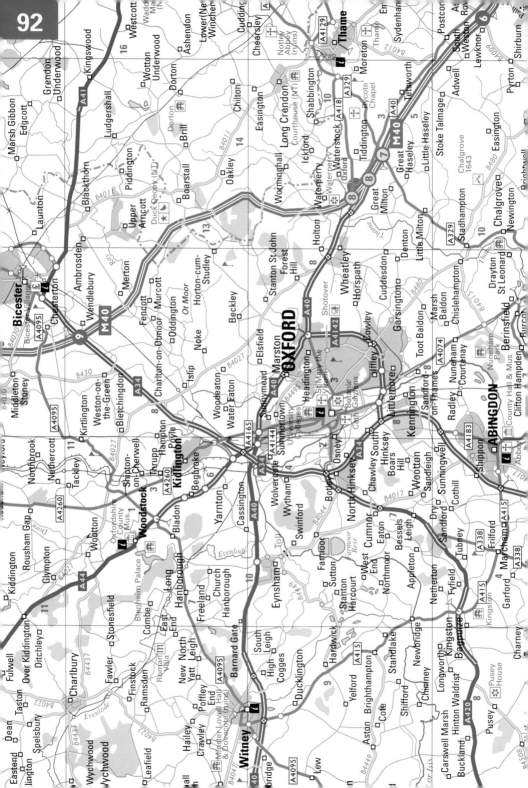

OXFORD | Oxfordshire | STD Code 01865

OXFORD

100   0   500yds
100   0   500m

Crown Copyright Reserved

TOURIST INFORMATION ☎ 01865 726871
THE OLD SCHOOL, GLOUCESTER GREEN,
OXFORD, OXFORDSHIRE, OX1 2DA

HOSPITAL A & E ☎ 01865 741166
JOHN RADCLIFFE HOSPITAL, HEADLEY WAY,
HEADINGTON, OXFORD, OX3 9DU

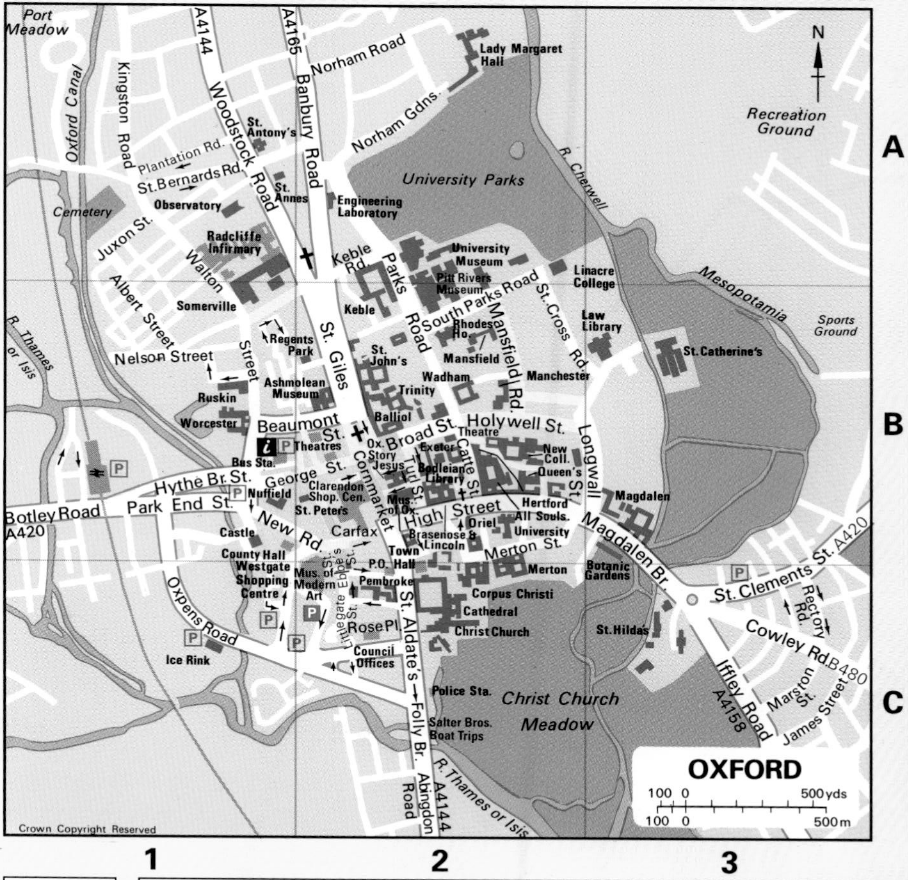

COUNCIL OFFICE ☎ 01865 249811
COUNCIL OFFICES, ST. ALDATES CHAMBERS,
OXFORD, OX1 1DS

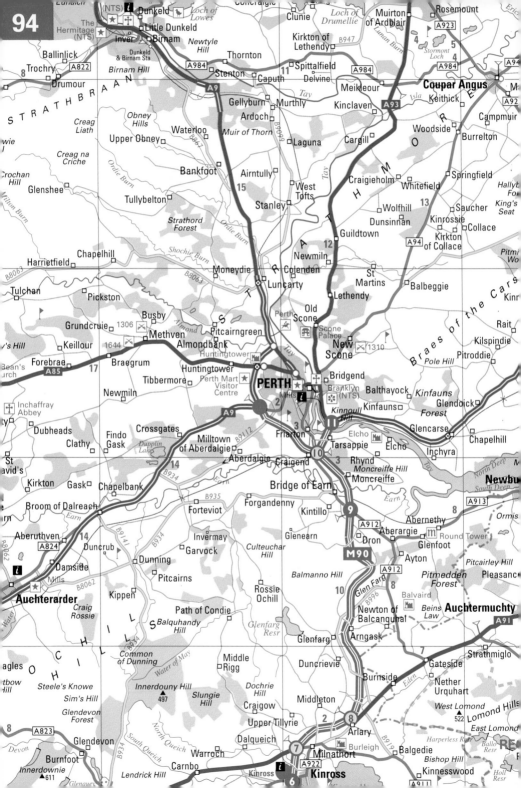

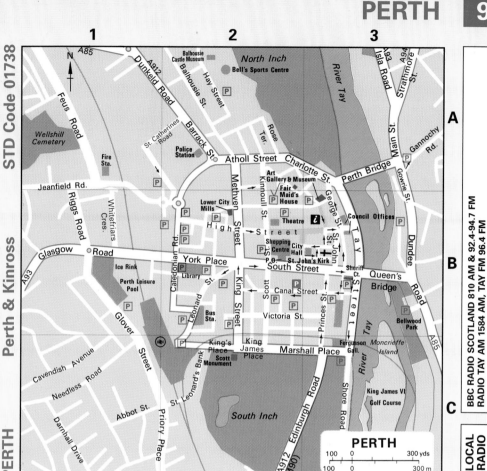

STD Code 01738

Perth & Kinross

PERTH

BBC RADIO SCOTLAND 810 AM & 92.4-94.7 FM
RADIO TAY AM 1584 AM, TAY FM 96.4 FM

LOCAL RADIO

TOURIST INFORMATION ☎ **01738 638353**
45 HIGH STREET, PERTH, PH1 5TJ

HOSPITAL A & E ☎ **01738 623311**
PERTH ROYAL INFIRMARY,
TAYMOUNT TERRACE, PERTH, PH1 1NX

COUNCIL OFFICE ☎ **01738 475000**
PERTH & KINROSS COUNCIL, PO BOX 77,
2 HIGH STREET, PERTH, PH1 5PH

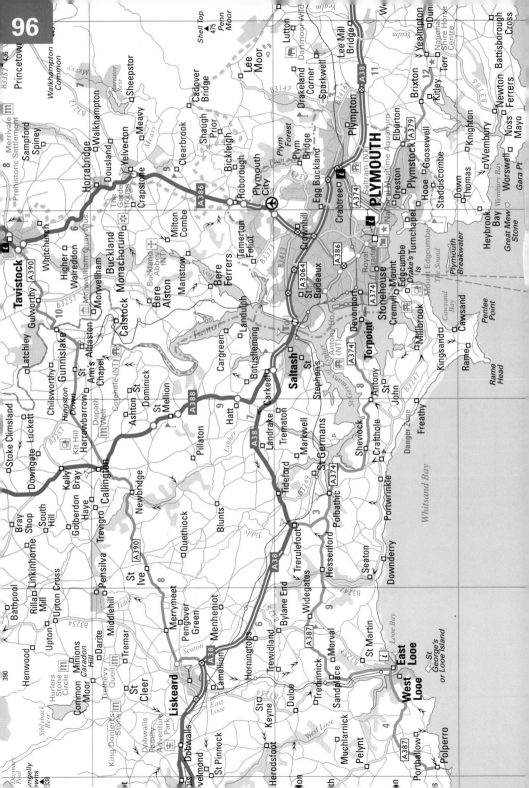

STD Code 01752 · Devon · PLYMOUTH

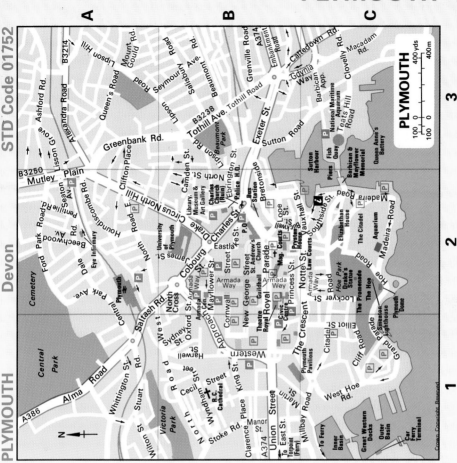

Crown Copyright Reserved

LOCAL RADIO

BBC RADIO DEVON 103.4 FM
PLYMOUTH SOUND AM 1152 AM, PLYMOUTH SOUND FM 97 FM

TOURIST INFORMATION ☎ 01752 264849
ISLAND HOUSE, 9 THE BARBICAN, PLYMOUTH,
DEVON, PL1 2LS

HOSPITAL A & E ☎ 01752 777111
DERRIFORD HOSPITAL, DERRIFORD ROAD,
CROWNHILL, PLYMOUTH, PL6 8DH

COUNCIL OFFICE ☎ 01752 668000
CIVIC CENTRE, ARMADA WAY,
PLYMOUTH, PL1 2EW

STD Code 023

PORTSMOUTH

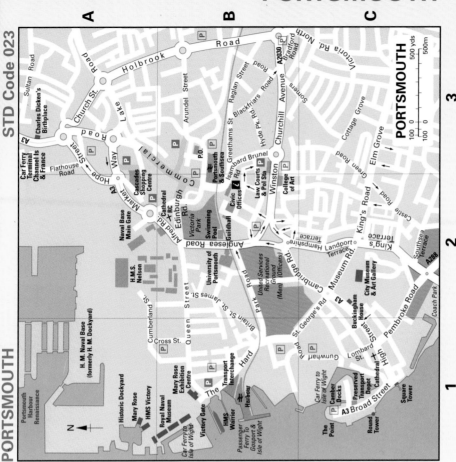

PORTSMOUTH

Alfred Road	B2	Hope Street	A2
Anglesea Road	B2	Hyde Park Road	B3
Arundel Street	B3	Isambard Brunel Road	B2
Blackfriars Road	B3	King's Road	C2
Bradford Road	B3	King's Terrace	C2
Britain Street	B1	Lake Road	A3
Broad Street	C1	Landport Terrace	C2
Cambridge Road	C2	Lombard Street	C1
Castle Road	C2	Market Way	A2
Church Street	A3	Museum Road	C2
Commercial Road	B2	Park Road	B2
Cottage Grove	C3	Pembroke Road	C1
Cross Street	B1	Queen Street	B1
Cumberland Street	A1	Raglan Street	B3
Edinburgh Road	B2	St. George's Road	C3
Elm Grove	C3	St. James Street	B2
Flathouse Road	A3	Somers Road	C3
Green Road	C2	Southsea Terrace	C2
Greetham Street	B3	Sultan Road	A3
Gunwharf Road	C1	The Hard	B1
Hampshire Terrace	C2	Victoria Road North	C3
High Street	C1	Winston Churchill	B2
Holbrook Road	A3	Avenue	

LOCAL RADIO

BBC RADIO SOLENT 96.1 FM
CAPITAL GOLD 1170 AM, OCEAN FM 97.5 FM, WAVE 105.2 FM

TOURIST INFORMATION ☎ 023 9282 6722
THE HARD, PORTSMOUTH, PO1 3QJ

HOSPITAL A & E ☎ 023 9228 6000
QUEEN ALEXANDRA HOSPITAL, SOUTHWICK
HILL ROAD, COSHAM, PORTSMOUTH, PO6 3LY

COUNCIL OFFICE ☎ 023 9282 2251
CIVIC OFFICES, GUILDHALL SQUARE,
PORTSMOUTH, PO1 2AL

Wallingford
North Moreton
South Moreton
Cholsey
Aston Upthorpe
Aston Tirrold
Crowmarsh Gifford
Cholsey & Wallingford Rly
North Stoke
Moulsford
South Stoke
Cleeve
Streatley
Goring
Aldworth
Basildon
Beale Park
Basildon Park (NT)
Ashampstead
Upper Basildon
Pangbourne
Yattendon
Frilsham
Bradfield
Englefield
Tidmarsh
Sulham
Tilehurst
North Street
Calcot
Theale
Southend
Chapel Row
Beenham
Beenham Hill
Midgham
Woolhampton
Midgham Sta.
Aldermaston Wharf
Aldermaston
Wasing
Aldermaston Soke
Padworth
Ufton Nervet
Sulhamstead
Sheffield Bottom
Burghfield
Burghfield Hill
Burghfield Common
Mortimer
Mortimer West End
Mortimer Sta.
Stratfield Mortimer
Heath End
Pamber
Roman City Walls
Stratfield Saye
Wellington
Cookley Green
Park Corner
Nuffield
Hailey
Ipsden
Huntercombe End
Nettlebed
Highmoor Cross
Stoke Row
Checkendon
Woodcote
Exlade Street
Cray's Pond
Rotherfield Peppard
Gallowstree Common
Cane End
Whitchurch Hill
Whitchurch
Toll
Purley on Thames
Mapledurham
Mapledurham House & Mill
Tokers Green
Kidmore End
Sonning Common
Caversham
Emmer Green
Dunsden Green
Museum of Reading
READING
Whitley
Three Mile Cross
Grazeley
Spencers Wood
Wokefield Park
Beech Hill
Riseley
Swallowfield
Swallowfield Park
Farley Hill
Shinfield
Russell's Water
Maidensgrove
Stonor
Stonor Park
Fawley
Middle Assendon
Bix
Lower Assendon
Shepherd's Green
Greys Court (NT)
Greys Green
Rotherfield Greys
Henley-on-Thames
River & Rowing Mus
Harpsden
Lower Shiplake
Shiplake
Binfield Heath
Sonning Eye
Play Hatch
Sonning
Woodley
Dinton Pastures
Winnersh
Sindlesham
Wokingham
Arborfield
Arborfield Cross
Barkham
Arborfield Garrison
California
Eversley
Finchampstead
Wick Hill
Sandhurst
Frieth
Skirmett
Rockwell End
Lower Woodend
Hambleden
Greenlands
Fawley Court
Mill End
Aston
Remenham
Remenham Hill
Medmenham
Hurley
Hurley Bottom
Thames or Isis
Burchett's Green
Ashley Hill
Cockpole Green
Crazies Hill
Warren Row
Knowl Hill
Wargrave
Kiln Green
Hare Hatch
Ruscombe
Twyford
Whistley Green
Hurst
Shurlock Row
Waltham St Lawrence
Littlewick Green
White Waltham
Woodlands Park
Paley Street
Binfield
Popeswood
Eastheath
Easthampstead
Crowthorne
Look Out Discovery Park
Surrey Hill
Bagshot
Marlow
Little Marlow
Flackwell Heath
Well End
Bourne End
Wooburn
Wooburn Green
Hedsor
Odds Farm Park
Bisham
Bisham Abbey N.S.C.
Priory
Cookham
Cookham Dean
Cookham Rise
Furze Platt
Pinkneys Green
Dropmore
Cliveden (NT)
Burnham Beeches
Taplow
Hitcham
Burnham
MAIDENHEAD
Bray Wick
Bray
Dorney
Dorney Court
Boveney
Eton Wick
Clewer Village
Windsor
WINDSOR
Stud Green
Holyport
Fifield
Oakley Green
Touchen-End
Legoland
Hawthorn Hill
Windsor Forest
Maiden's Green
Cranbourne
Warfield
Winkfield
Newell Green
Winkfield Row
Woodside
BRACKNELL
North Ascot
Ascot
Burleigh
Cheapside
South Ascot
Sunninghill
Sunningdale
Windlesham
Lightwater
Burrowhill
Farnham Common
Farnham Royal
Salt Hill
A4130
A417
A329
A340
A4074
A4155
A4130
A321
A4
A329(M)
A404(M)
A404
A4094
A308
A330
A3095
A322
A332
A327
A33
A30
M4
M3
B4009
B4526
B471
B481
B480
B482
B4447
B3024
B3018
B3034
B3350
B3270
B3349
B3030
B3430
B3348
B3022
B3020
B383
B386

STD Code 0118

READING

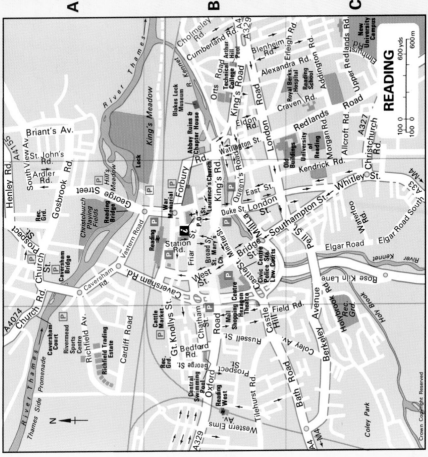

Street Index

LOCAL RADIO

BBC THAMES VALLEY FM 104.4 FM
CLASSIC GOLD 1431 1431 AM, 2-TEN FM 97 FM

TOURIST INFORMATION ☎ 0118 956 6226
TOWN HALL, BLAGRAVE STREET,
READING, RG1 1QH

HOSPITAL A & E ☎ 0118 987 5111
ROYAL BERKSHIRE HOSPITAL, LONDON ROAD,
READING, RG1 5AN

COUNCIL OFFICE ☎ 0118 939 0900
CIVIC CENTRE, CIVIC OFFICES, (OFF CASTLE ST.)
READING, RG1 7TD

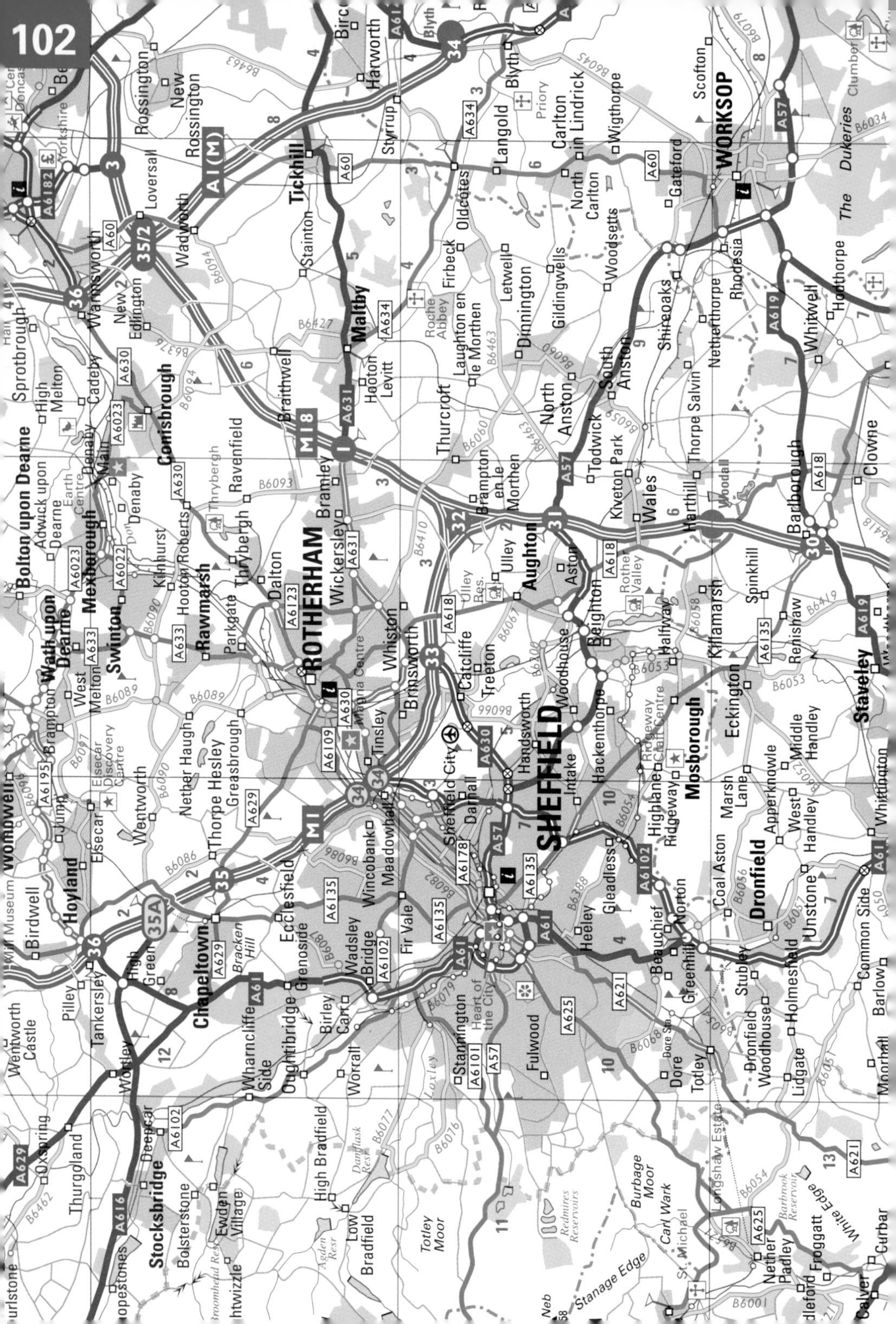

SHEFFIELD
ROTHERHAM
WORKSOP
Rossington
New Rossington
Loversall
Wadworth
Tickhill
Harworth
Styrrup
Blyth
Langold
Carlton in Lindrick
North Carlton
Oldcotes
Wigthorpe
Scofton
Gateford
Clumber
The Dukeries
Warmsworth
Edlington
New Edlington
Stainton
Maltby
Roche Abbey
Firbeck
Letwell
Laughton en le Morthen
Dinnington
Gildingwells
Woodsetts
Shireoaks
Rhodesia
Netherthorpe
Whitwell
Hodthorpe
Sprotbrough
High Melton
Cadeby
Conisbrough
Braithwell
Hooton Levitt
Thurcroft
North Anston
South Anston
Thorpe Salvin
Todwick
Kiveton Park
Wales
Harthill
Barlborough
Clowne
Bolton upon Dearne
Adwick upon Dearne
Denaby Main
Denaby
Earth Centre
Mexborough
Ravenfield
Thrybergh
Bramley
Brampton en le Morthen
Ulley
Aughton
Aston
Rother Valley
Spinkhill
Wath upon Dearne
Swinton
Kilnhurst
Hooton Roberts
Rawmarsh
Parkgate
Dalton
Wickersley
Whiston
Treeton
Catcliffe
Beighton
Woodhouse
Halfway
Killamarsh
Renishaw
West Melton
Brampton
Wombwell
Jump
Elsecar
Wentworth
Nether Haugh
Thorpe Hesley
Greasbrough
Magna Centre
Tinsley
Brinsworth
Sheffield City
Handsworth
Hackenthorpe
Mosborough
Eckington
Middle Handley
Staveley
Hoyland
Birdwell
Chapeltown
Ecclesfield
Wincobank
Meadowhall
Darnall
Intake
Highlane
Ridgeway
Marsh Lane
Apperknowle
West Handley
Whittington
Pilley
Tankersley
High Green
Bracken Hill
Grenoside
Wadsley Bridge
Fir Vale
Heeley
Gleadless
Norton
Coal Aston
Dronfield
Unstone
Common Side
Wentworth Castle
Wortley
Wharncliffe Side
Oughtibridge
Birley Carr
Worrall
Stannington
Heart of the City
Fulwood
Beauchief
Greenhill
Stubley
Holmesfield
Barlow
Dore
Totley
Dronfield Woodhouse
Lidgate
Moorhall
Oxspring
Thurgoland
Deepcar
Stocksbridge
Bolsterstone
Ewden Village
High Bradfield
Low Bradfield
Damflask Resr.
Agden Resr
Totley Moor
Redmires Reservoirs
Burbage Moor
Carl Wark
Stanage Edge
Longshaw Estate
St. Michael
Nether Padley
Froggatt
Curbar
Calver
Barbrook Reservoir
White Edge
Broomhead Resr
Loxley
M1
M18
A1(M)
A57
A61
A60
A630
A631
A618
A619
A616
A629
A621
A625
A6135
A6102
A6109
A6123
A6178
A6101
A634
A6023
A6022
A6195
A6182

STD Code 0114   **South Yorkshire**   **SHEFFIELD**

A   B   C

1   2   3

SHEFFIELD

300 yds
300m

Street	Grid	Street	Grid
Allen Street	A2	Flat Street	B3
Angel Street	A3	Furnace Hill	A2
Arundel Gate	B3	Furnival Gate	B2
Arundel Street	C2	Furnival Street	C2
Bank Street	A3	Furnival Street	C2
Barker's Pool	B2	Gell Street	B1
Best Street	A1	Gibraltar Street	A2
Blonk Street	A3	Glossop Road	B1
Bridge Street	A3	Granville Road	B3
Broad Lane	B1	Hanover Way	C1
Broomhall	C1	Harmer Lane	B3
Street		Haymarket	A3
Brown Street	C3	Headford Street	C1
Campo Lane	A2	High Street	A3
Carver Street	B2	Howard Street	B3
Castle Square	A3	Hoyle Street	A1
Castlegate	A3	Leadmill Road	C3
Cavendish	B1	Leopold Street	B2
Street		Mappin Street	B1
Charles Street	B3	Matilda Street	C3
Charter Row	C2	Meadow Street	A1
Charter Square	B2	Moore Street	C1
Church Street	A2	Netherthorpe	A2
Commercial	A3	Road	
Street		Norfolk Street	B3
Corporation	A2	Nursery Street	A3
Street		Pinstone Street	B2
Devonshire	B1	Pond Hill	B3
Street		Pond Street	B3
Division Street	B2	Portobello	B1
Dover Street	A1	Street	
Ecclesall Road	C1	Queen Street	A2
Eldon Street	B2	Rockingham	B2
Exchange Street	A3	Street	
Eyre Lane	C2	Russell Street	A2
Eyre Street	C2	Scotland Street	A2
Fitzwilliam	B1	Sheaf Square	C2
Street		Sheaf Street	B3
Shepherd Street	A2	Trippet Lane	B2
Shoreham	C3	Upper Allen	A1
Street		Street	
Shrewsbury	C3	Upper Hanover	B1
Road		Street	
Sidney Street	C2	Waingate	A3
Snig Hill	A3	Wellington	B2
Solly Street	A1	Street	
St. Mary's Gate	C2	West Bar	A2
St. Mary's Road	C2	West Street	B2
St. Philip's Road	A1	Westbar Green	A2
Suffolk Road	C3	Weston Street	A1
Surrey Street	B2		
Tenter Street	A2		
The Moor	C2		
Thomas Street	C1		
Townhead	A2		
Street			

LOCAL RADIO

BBC RADIO SHEFFIELD 104.1 FM
MAGIC AM, SOUTH YORKSHIRE 1548 AM, HALLAM FM 97.4 FM

TOURIST INFORMATION ☎ 0114 273 4671/2
PEACE GARDENS, SHEFFIELD,
SOUTH YORKSHIRE, S1 2HH

HOSPITAL A & E ☎ 0114 243 4343
NORTHERN GENERAL HOSPITAL, HERRIES ROAD,
SHEFFIELD, S5 7AU

COUNCIL OFFICE ☎ 0114 272 6444
TOWN HALL, PINSTONE STREET,
SHEFFIELD, S1 2HH

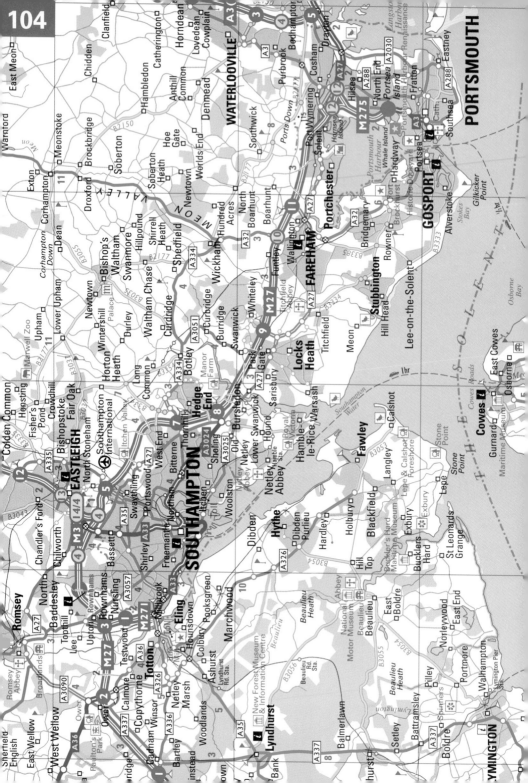

STD Code 023

SOUTHAMPTON

SOUTHAMPTON

Map index:

Above Bar Street	B2
Albert Road North	C3
Bedford Place	A1
Belvidere Road	B3
Bernard Street	C2
Brintons Road	A2
Briton Street	C2
Canute Road	C2
Castle Way	B2
Central Bridge	C2
Central Road	C2
Chapel Road	B1
Civic Centre Road	A2
Clovelly Road	A1
Commercial Road	A2
Cranbury Avenue	A1
Cumberland Place	A1
Derby Road	A3
Dorset Street	A2
East Park Terrace	B2
East Street	B2
Harbour Parade	B1
Herbert Walker Avenue	B1
High Street	B2
Howard Road	A1
Kingsway	B2
Landguard Road	A1
London Road	A2

Marine Parade	B3
Marsh Lane	B2
Millbank Street	A3
Morris Road	A1
Mount Pleasant Road	A3
New Road	B2
Northam Road	A3
Ocean Way	C2
Onslow Road	A2
Oxford Street	B2
Palmerston Road	C2
Platform Road	C2
Portland Terrace	B1
Prince's Street	A3
Queen's Way	C2
Radcliffe Road	A3
St. Andrews Road	A2
St. Mary's Road	A2
St. Mary Street	B2
Shirley Road	A1
Solent Road	B1
Southern Road	B1
Terminus Terrace	C2
Town Quay	C1
Trafalgar Road	C2
West Quay Road	B1
West Road	C2
Western Esplanade	B1
Wilton Avenue	A1

TOURIST INFORMATION ☎ 023 8022 1106
9 CIVIC CENTRE ROAD,
SOUTHAMPTON, SO14 7JP

HOSPITAL A & E ☎ 023 8077 7222
SOUTHAMPTON GENERAL HOSP, TREMONA RD,
SHIRLEY, SOUTHAMPTON, SO16 6YD

COUNCIL OFFICE ☎ 023 8022 3855
CIVIC CENTRE, CIVIC CENTRE ROAD,
SOUTHAMPTON, SO14 7LY

LOCAL RADIO

BBC RADIO SOLENT 96.1 FM
CAPITAL GOLD 1557 AM, POWER FM 103.2 FM, WAVE 105.2 FM

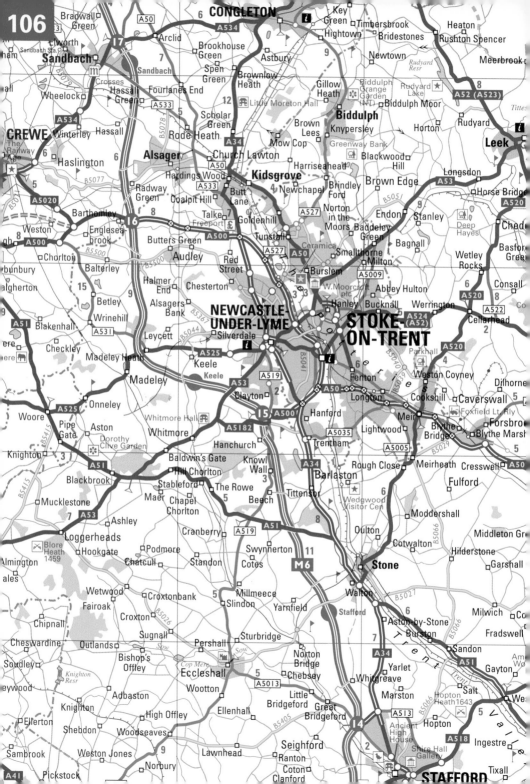

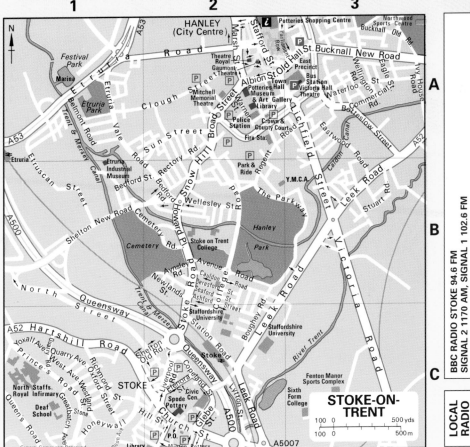

STD Code 01782

STOKE-ON-TRENT

BBC RADIO STOKE 94.6 FM
SIGNAL 2 1170 AM, SIGNAL 1 102.6 FM

LOCAL RADIO

Albion Street	A2	Clough Street	A2	Ivy House Road	A3	Shelton New Road	B1
Ashford Street	B2	College Road	C2	Leek Road	C2	Shelton Old Road	C1
Avenue Road	B2	Commercial Road	A3	Lichfield Street	A3	Snow Hill	B2
Aynsley Road	B2	Copeland Street	C2	Liverpool Road	C2	Stafford Street	A2
Bedford Road	B2	Eagle Street	A3	Lytton Street	C2	Station Road	C2
Bedford Street	B1	Eastwood Road	A3	Marsh Street	A2	Stoke	C2
Belmont Road	A1	Elenora Street	C2	Newlands Street	B2	Stoke Road	C2
Beresford Street	B2	Etruria Road	A1	North Street	B1	Stone	C1
Boon Avenue	C1	Etruria Vale Road	A1	Old Hall Street	A2	Stuart Road	B3
Botteslow Street	A3	Etruscan Street	A1	Oxford Street	C1	Sun Street	A2
Boughey Road	C2	Glebe Street	C2	Parliament Row	A2	The Parkway	B2
Broad Street	A2	Greatbatch Avenue	C1	Prince's Road	C1	Victoria Road	B3
Bucknall New Road	A3	Hanley	A2	Quarry Avenue	C1	Warner Street	A2
Bucknall Old Road	A3	Hartshill Road	C1	Quarry Road	C1	Waterloo Street	A3
Cauldon Road	B2	Hill Street	C2	Queen's Road	C1	Wellesley Street	B2
Cemetery Road	B1	Honeywall	C1	Queensway	B1	Wellington Road	A3
Church Street	C2	Howard Place	B2	Rectory Road	B2	West Avenue	C1
				Regent Road	B2	Westland Street	C1
				Richmond Street	C1	Yoxall Avenue	C1
				Seaford Street	B2		

TOURIST INFORMATION ☎ 01782 236000
POTTERIES SHOPPING CENTRE, QUADRANT RD,
STOKE-ON-TRENT, ST1 1RZ

HOSPITAL A & E ☎ 01782 715444
NORTH STAFFORDSHIRE ROYAL INFIRMARY,
PRINCE'S ROAD, STOKE-ON-TRENT, ST4 7LN

COUNCIL OFFICE ☎ 01782 234567
TOWN HALL, CIVIC CENTRE, GLEBE STREET,
STOKE-ON-TRENT, ST4 1HH

Southam

A4

ROYAL LEAMINGTON SPA

Wappenbury · Eathorpe · Cubbington · Hunningham · Weston under Wetherley · Offchurch · Radford Semele · Ufton · Harbury · Chesterton Green · Bishop's Itchington · Gaydon · Northend · Knightcote · Burton Dassett Hills · Fenny Compton · Avon Dassett · Farnborough · Horley · Hornton · Wroxton

Ashow · Old Milverton · Whitnash · Bishop's Tachbrook · Warwick · Moreton Morrell · Wellesbourne · Kineton · Little Kineton · Combrook · Butlers Marston · Pillerton Hersey · Pillerton Priors · Radway · Edgehill · Ratley · Upton · Shenington · Alkerton

Leek Wootton · Hatton · Shrewley · Haseley · Budbrooke · Hampton on the Hill · Norton Lindsey · Sherbourne · Barford · Hampton Lucy · Charlecote · Loxley · Ettington · Fulready · Halford · Idlicote · Tredington · Honington · Middle Tysoe · Brook Cottage · Lower Tysoe · Upper Tysoe · Whatcote · Oxhill

Warwick · Longbridge · Wasperton · Alveston · Stratford-upon-Avon · Walton · Alderminster · Newbold on Stour · Armscote · Blackwell · Darlingscott

Rowington · Pinley Green · Preston Bagot · Claverdon · Langley · Edstone · Bearley · Snitterfield · Ingon · Tiddington · Shottery · Clifford Chambers · Atherstone on Stour · Preston on Stour · Wimpstone · Lower Quinton · Upper Quinton · Ilmington · Hidcote Manor · Mickleton

Lowsonford · Henley-in-Arden · Beaudesert · Wootton Wawen · Aston Cantlow · Wilmcote · Haselor · Billesley · Temple Grafton · Binton · Luddington · Dorsington · Long Marston · Pebworth · Honeybourne

Ullenhall · Oldberrow · Morton Bagot · Great Alne · Little Alne · Walcote · Red Hill · Oversley Green · Exhall · Wixford · Ardens Grafton · Bidford-on-Avon · Barton · Welford-on-Avon · Cleeve Prior · North Littleton · Middle Littleton · South Littleton · Bretforton · Badsey

Tanworth in Arden · Gorcott Hill · Mappleborough Green · Studley · Coughton · King's Coughton · Alcester · Arrow · Ragley Hall · Dunnington · Iron Cross · Salford Priors · Abbots Salford · Harvington · Norton · Aldington · Evesham

REDDITCH · Beoley End · Walkwood · Crabbs Cross · Hunt End · Studley Common · Sambourne · Cookhill · New End · Feckenham · Weethley · Abbots Morton · Rous Lench · Atch Lench · Church Lench · Twyford · Middle Littleton · Offenham

STRATFORD-UPON-AVON Warwickshire STD Code 01789

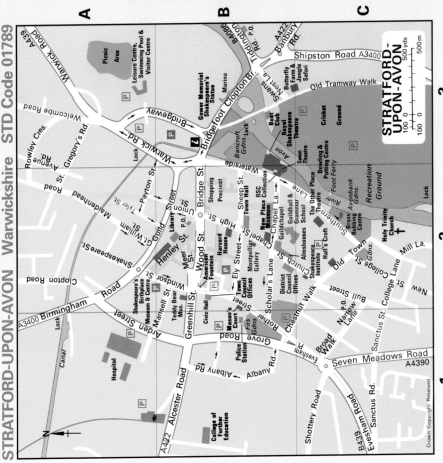

LOCAL RADIO

BBC RADIO COVENTRY & WARWICKSHIRE 94.8 & 103.7 FM
102 FM - THE BEAR 102 FM

TOURIST INFORMATION ☎ 01789 293127
BRIDGEFOOT, STRATFORD-UPON-AVON,
WARWICKSHIRE, CV37 6GW

HOSPITAL A & E ☎ 01789 205831
STRATFORD-UPON-AVON HOSPITAL, ARDEN ST,
STRATFORD-UPON-AVON, CV37 6NX

COUNCIL OFFICE ☎ 01789 267575
COUNCIL OFFICES, ELIZABETH HOUSE,
CHURCH ST, STRATFORD-UPON-AVON, CV37 6HX

STD Code 01792

SWANSEA

Scale: 500yds / 500m / 100 / 0

Map labels include:
Foxhole Rd., River Tawe (Afon Tawe), Neath Road, B4603, Pentre Guinea Rd., East Bankway, Morris Lane, Morris St., Mackworth St., Delhi St., A483, Fabian Way, Prince of Wales Dock, Entrance Channel, New Cut Road, High Street, Llangyfelach Rd., Carmarthen Road, A483, Dyfatty, Park, Dyfatty St., New Orchard Street, Hill Rd., Alexandra Rd., Grove Pl., Orchard St., Police Sta., Castle St., Swansea Castle, Old Guildhall, Burrows Rd., Somerset Pl., Cambrian Pl., Museum, Burrows Pl., Maritime & Industrial Museum, Wind St., Leisure Centre, St. David's Sq. Shopping Centre, Marina, Swansea Bay, Glyn Vivian Art Gallery, Technical College, Library, Mount Pleasant, North Hill, Waun-wen Rd., Townhill Rd., Mayhill Rd., Rec. Grd., Islwyn Rd., Cromwell St., Terrace Rd., Mayhill Gdns., Constitution Hill, Brooklands Terrace, Hanover St., Rose, Pen-y-Craig Rd., Gwent Rd., Powys Avenue, Dyfed Avenue, Gors Avenue, Terrace, Westbury St., Walter Rd., A4118, Princess Way, Kingsway, The Kingsway, Mansel Street, Page St., De La Beche St., Grand Theatre, Quadrant Shopping Centre, Mkt., Singleton St., Bus Depot, Oxford St., West Way, Clarence St., St. Helen's Road, Beach St., Bond St., Law Courts St., Swansea City A.F.C. Ground, Argyle St., Vincent St., Glamorgan St., Tower, Oystermouth Road, County Hall, St. Helen's Avenue, Brynymor Rd., Brynmill Cres., Victoria Pk., King Edward's Rd., Guildhall & Brangwyn Hall, South Guildhall Rd., Mumbles Swimming Baths, Westbury St., A4067, Walter Road

LOCAL RADIO

BBC RADIO WALES 882 AM
SWANSEA SOUND 1170 AM, 96.4 THE WAVE 96.4 FM

TOURIST INFORMATION ☎ 01792 468321
WEST WAY CAR PARK, SWANSEA, SA1 3QG

HOSPITAL A & E ☎ 01792 702222
MORRISTON HOSPITAL, MORRISTON,
SWANSEA, SA6 6NL

COUNCIL OFFICE ☎ 01792 636000
THE GUILDHALL, (OFF FRANCIS STREET),
SWANSEA, SA1 4PA

STD Code 01793

SWINDON

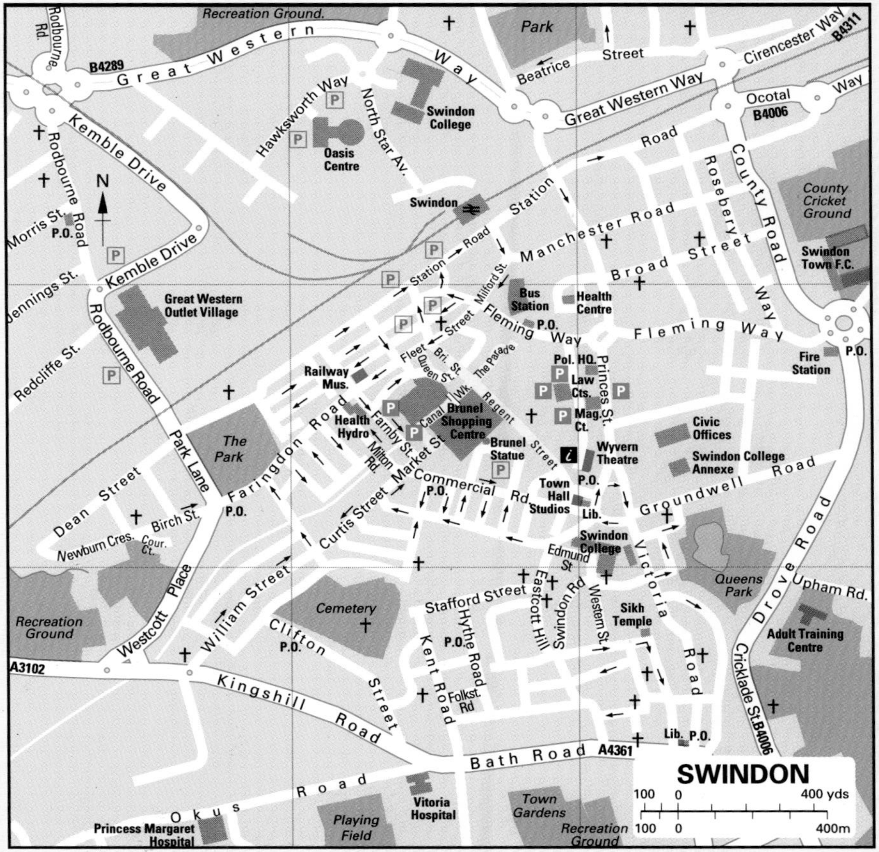

LOCAL RADIO

BBC WILTSHIRE SOUND 103.6 FM
BRUNEL CLASSIC GOLD 936 AM, GWR FM WILTSHIRE 97.2 FM

TOURIST INFORMATION ☎ 01793 530328
37 REGENT STREET, SWINDON, SN1 1JL

HOSPITAL A & E ☎ 01793 536231
PRINCESS MARGARET HOSPITAL, OKUS ROAD,
SWINDON, SN1 4JU

COUNCIL OFFICE ☎ 01793 463000
CIVIC OFFICES, EUCLID STREET, SWINDON,
SN1 2JH

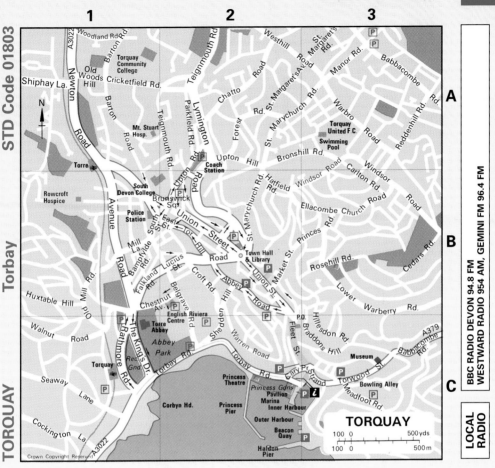

STD Code 01803

Torbay

TORQUAY

BBC RADIO DEVON 94.8 FM
WESTWARD RADIO 954 AM, GEMINI FM 96.4 FM

LOCAL RADIO

TORQUAY

Abbey Road	B2	Croft Road	B2	Mill Lane	B1	Strand	C3
Avenue Road	B1	East Street	B2	Newton Road	A1	Teignmouth Road	A2
Babbacombe Road	C3	Ellacombe Church		Old Mill Road	B1	The King's Drive	C1
Bampfylde Road	B1	Road	B3	Old Woods Hill	A1	Torbay Road	C2
Barton Road	A1	Falkland Road	B1	Parkfield Road	A2	Tor Hill Road	B2
Belgrave Road	B2	Fleet Street	C2	Prince's Road	B3	Torwood Street	C3
Braddons Hill	C3	Forest Road	A2	Rathmore Road	C1	Union Street	B2
Bronshill Road	A2	Hatfield Road	B2	Reddenhill Road	A3	Upton Hill	A2
Brunswick Square	B2	Hillesdon Road	C3	Rosehill Road	B3	Upton Road	B2
Carlton Road	A3	Huxtable Hill	B1	St. Margaret's Avenue	A2	Walnut Road	C1
Cary Parade	C2	Lower Warberry Road	B3	St. Margaret's Road	A2	Warbro Road	A3
Cedars Road	B3	Lucius Street	B2	St. Marychurch Road	B2	Warren Road	C2
Chatto Road	A2	Lymington Road	A2	Seaway Lane	C1	Westhill Road	A2
Chestnut Avenue	B1	Manor Road	A3	Shedden Hill	C2	Windsor Road	B3
Cockington Lane	C1	Market Street	B2	Shiphay Lane	A1		
Cricketfield Road	A1	Meadfoot Road	C3	South Street	B1		

TOURIST INFORMATION ☎ 01803 297428
VAUGHAN PARADE, TORQUAY, TQ2 5JG

HOSPITAL A & E ☎ 01803 614567
TORBAY HOSPITAL, LAWES BRIDGE,
TORQUAY, TQ2 7AA

COUNCIL OFFICE ☎ 01803 201201
CIVIC OFFICES, CASTLE CIRCUS,
TORQUAY, TQ1 3DR

STD Code 01962

Hampshire

WINCHESTER

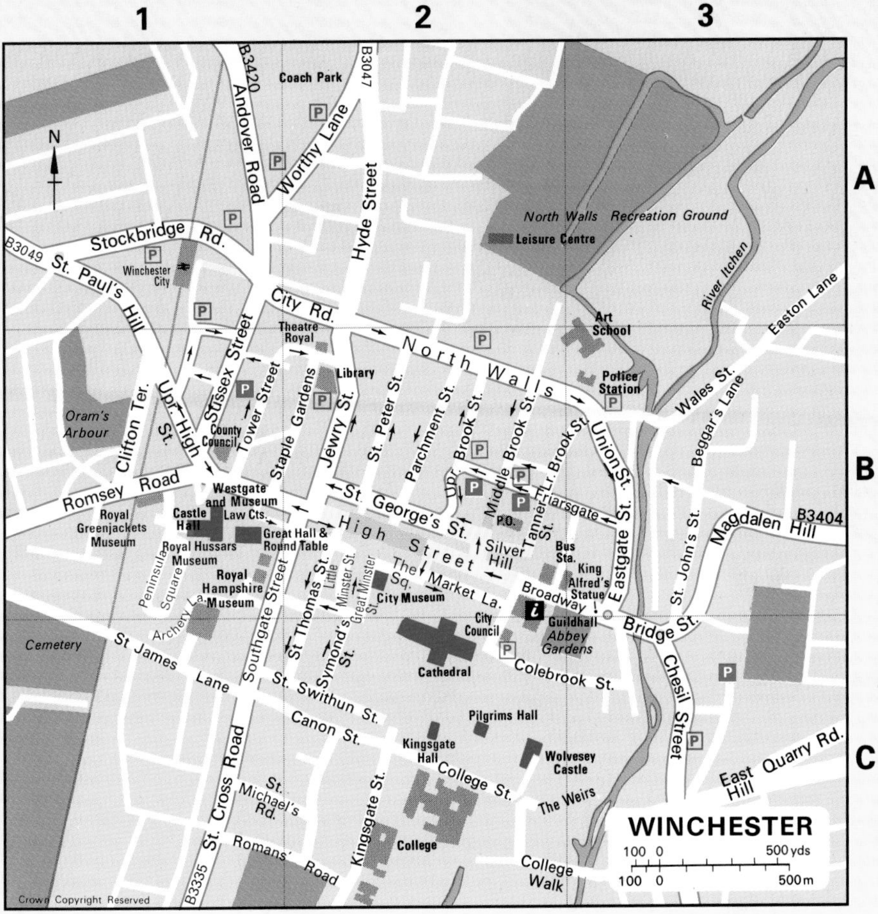
1
2
3
A
B
C
N
Coach Park
B3420
Andover Road
B3047
Worthy Lane
Hyde Street
North Walls Recreation Ground
Leisure Centre
River Itchen
Easton Lane
Stockbridge Rd.
B3049
St. Paul's Hill
Winchester City
City Rd.
Theatre Royal
North Walls
Art School
Police Station
Wales St.
Beggar's Lane
Library
Oram's Arbour
Clifton Ter.
Upr. High St.
Sussex Street
Tower Street
County Council
Staple Gardens
Jewry St.
St. Peter St.
Parchment St.
Upr. Brook St.
Middle Brook St.
Lr. Brook St.
Union St.
Tanner St.
Friarsgate
Eastgate St.
St. John's St.
Magdalen Hill
B3404
Romsey Road
Westgate and Museum
Law Cts.
Castle Hall
Royal Greenjackets Museum
Great Hall & Round Table
Royal Hussars Museum
St. George's St.
P.O.
High Street
Silver Hill
Bus Sta.
King Alfred's Statue
Broadway
Bridge St.
Royal Hampshire Museum
Peninsula Square
Archery La.
Southgate Street
St Thomas St.
Little Minster St.
Great Minster St.
The Sq.
Market La.
City Museum
City Council
Guildhall
Abbey Gardens
Symond's St.
Cathedral
Colebrook St.
Cemetery
St James Lane
St. Swithun St.
Canon St.
Pilgrims Hall
Chesil Street
Kingsgate Hall
Wolvesey Castle
College St.
The Weirs
East Hill
East Quarry Rd.
St. Cross Road
St. Michael's Rd.
Kingsgate St.
College
Romans' Road
B3335
College Walk
WINCHESTER
100 0 500 yds
100 0 500 m
Crown Copyright Reserved

BBC RADIO SOLENT 96.1 FM
OCEAN FM 96.7 FM, WIN 107.2 FM

LOCAL RADIO

Andover Road	A1	East Hill	C3	Peninsula Square	B1	Southgate Street	C1
Archery Lane	C1	Friarsgate	B2	Quarry Road	C3	Staple Gardens	B1
Beggar's Lane	B3	Great Minster Street	B2	Romans' Road	C1	Stockbridge Road	A1
Bridge Stret	C3	High Street	B2	Romsey Road	B1	Sussex Street	B1
Broadway	B2	Hyde Street	A2	St. Cross Road	C1	Symond's Street	C2
Canon Street	C2	Jewry Street	B2	St. George's Street	B2	Tanner Street	B2
Chesil Street	C3	Kingsgate Street	C2	St. James Lane	C1	The Square	B2
City Road	A1	Little Minster Street	B2	St. John's Street	B3	Tower Street	B1
Clifton Terrace	B1	Lower Brook Street	B2	St. Michael's Road	C1	Union Street	B3
Colebrook Street	C2	Magdalen Hill	B3	St. Paul's Hill	A1	Upper Brook Street	B2
College Street	C2	Market Lane	B2	St. Peter Street	B2	Upper High Street	B1
College Walk	C2	Middle Brook Street	B2	St. Swithun Street	C2	Wales Street	B3
Eastgate Street	B3	North Walls	B2	St. Thomas Street	C2	Worthy Lane	A2
Easton Lane	A3	Parchment Street	B2	Silver Hill	B2		

TOURIST INFORMATION ☎ 01962 840500
GUILDHALL, THE BROADWAY, WINCHESTER
HAMPSHIRE, SO23 9LJ

HOSPITAL A & E ☎ 01962 863535
ROYAL HAMPSHIRE COUNTY HOSPITAL,
ROMSEY ROAD, WINCHESTER, SO22 5DG

COUNCIL OFFICE ☎ 01962 840222
CITY OFFICES, COLEBROOK STREET,
WINCHESTER, SO23 9LJ

WINDSOR **Windsor & Maidenhead** **STD Code 01753**

LOCAL RADIO

BBC THAMES VALLEY FM 95.4 FM
STAR FM 106.6 FM

WINDSOR

0 100   400 yds
0 100   400m

TOURIST INFORMATION ☎ 01753 743900
24 HIGH STREET, WINDSOR, SL4 1LH

HOSPITAL A & E ☎ 01753 633000
WEXHAM PARK HOSPITAL, WEXHAM STREET,
SLOUGH, SL2 4HL

COUNCIL OFFICE ☎ 01753 810525
COUNCIL OFFICES, YORK HOUSE,
SHEET STREET, WINDSOR, SL4 1DD

Map labels:

The Home Park Recreation Ground
Queen Mary's Doll House
The Home Park (Private)
Mausoleum (Queen Victoria & Prince Albert)
Windsor Castle
Royal Mews
Riverside Station
Municipal Offices
Y.W.C.A.
Datchet Rd
Windsor Bridge
High Street
Guildhall
Sheet St
Kings Road
South Meadow
Meadow Lane
The Brocas
River Thames
P.O.
Eton Council Offices
Central Station
Shopping Centre
Avenue
Tourist Reception Centre
Barry Avenue
Lib
Peascod St
P.O.
Victoria Barracks
Princess Margaret Hospital
Alexandra Road
Grove Road
Frances Road
Bolton Avenue
Bolton Road
Industrial Estate
Charles St
Clarence Road
St. Leonard's Road
East Berkshire Fire Station
King Edward VII Hospital
Osborne Road
Arthur Road
Oxford Road
Princess Christian's Hospital
Alma Road
Police Station
Combermere Barracks
St. Leonard's Road
Vansittart Road
Windsor Leisure Pool
Stovell Road
Eton and Windsor Relief Road
Sports Ground
Goslar Way
Clarence Rd
Green Lane
York Avenue
Bulkeley Avenue
Bolton Road
Racecourse
YHA
Ambulance Station
Parsonage Lane
Playing Field
Clarence Rd
Convent of St. John
Green Lane
Springfield Road
Imperial Road
Playing Field
Cemetery
A331
A332
A308
B3024
B3022
B3173
The Long Walk

STD Code 01905

Worcestershire

WORCESTER

BBC RADIO HEREFORD & WORCESTER 94.7 FM
CLASSIC GOLD 1530 AM, WYVERN FM 102.8 FM

LOCAL RADIO

WORCESTER

Angel Place	B1	Farrier Street	A1	Newport Street	B1	Shaw Street	B2
Angel Street	B2	Foregate Street	A2	New Road	C1	Shrub Hill	B3
Back Lane South	A1	Foundry Street	C3	New Street	B2	Shrub Hill Road	A3
Bath Road	C2	Friar Street	C2	North Quay	B1	Sidbury	C2
Bridge Street	B1	George Street	B3	Park Street	C3	Stanley Road	B3
Britannia Road	A1	High Street	B2	Pheasant Street	B2	Tallow Hill	B3
Broad Street	B1	Hill Street	B3	Pump Street	B2	The Butts	B1
Carden Street	C2	Hylton Road	B1	Rainbow Hill	A3	The Cross	B2
Castle Street	A1	Infirmary Walk	A1	St. Martin's Gate	B2	The Moors	A1
Chestnut Walk	A2	Kleve Walk	C1	St. Mary's Street	A2	The Shambles	B2
City Walls Road	C2	London Road	C2	St. Oswalds Road	A1	The Tything	A1
College Street	C2	Loves Grove	A1	St. Paul's Street	B3	Tolladine Road	A3
Copenhagen Street	B1	Lowesmoor	B2	Sansome Street	B2	Trinity Street	B2
Croft Road	B1	Lowesmoor Place	A2	Sansome Walk	A2	Upper Tything	A1
Deansway	B1	Midland Road	C3	Severn Street	C2	Wyld's Lane	C3
Dolday	B1	Moor Street	A1	Severn Terrace	A1		

TOURIST INFORMATION ☎ 01905 726311
THE GUILDHALL, HIGH STREET,
WORCESTER, WR1 2EY

HOSPITAL A & E ☎ 01905 763333
WORCESTER ROYAL INFIRMARY, RONKSWOOD
HOSPITAL, NEWTOWN ROAD, WR5 1HN

COUNCIL OFFICE ☎ 01905 723471
GUILDHALL, HIGH STREET,
WORCESTER, WR1 2EY

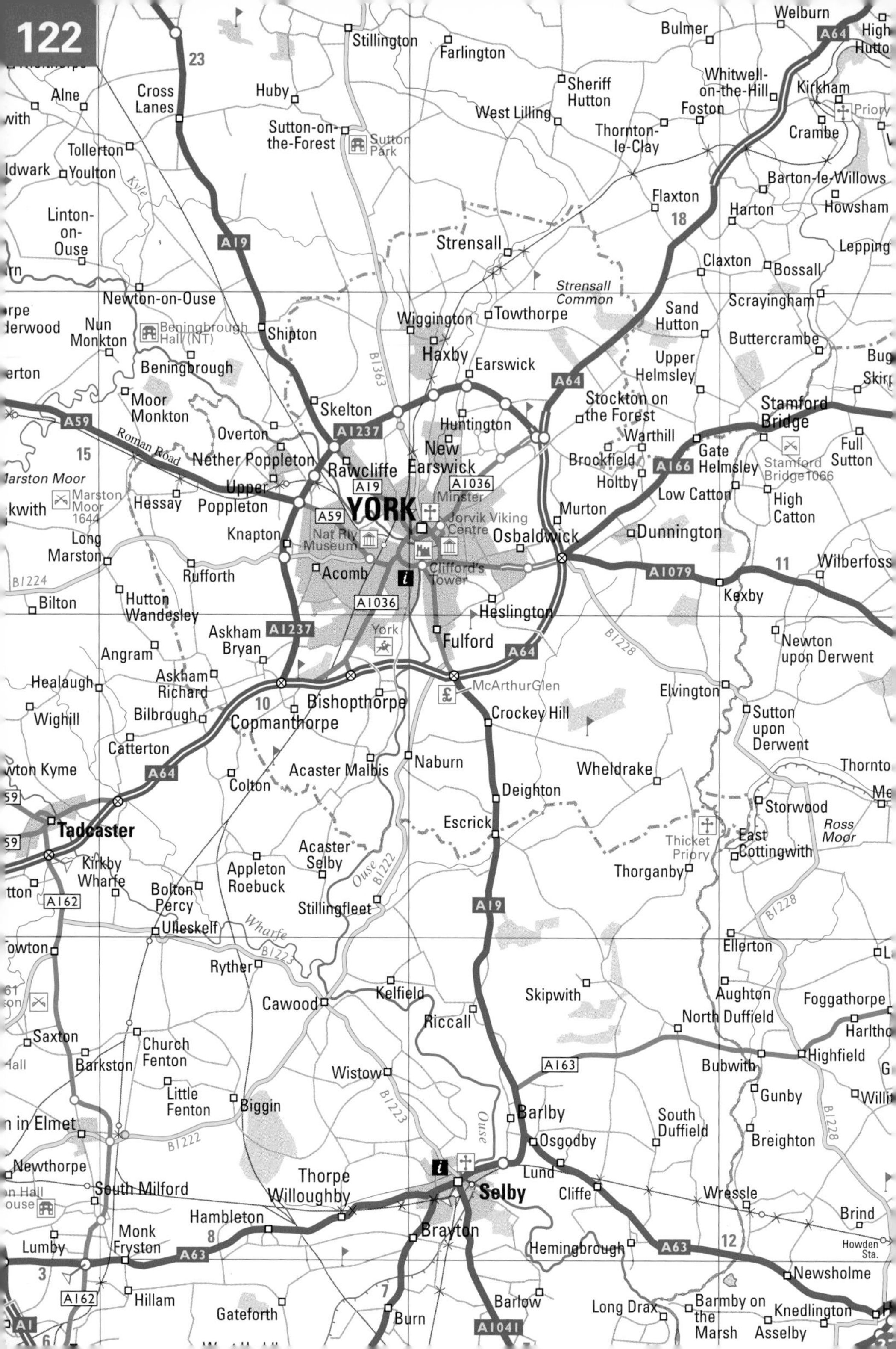
Welburn
Stillington
Farlington
Bulmer
A64
Alne
Cross Lanes
Huby
Sheriff Hutton
Whitwell-on-the-Hill
Kirkham
Priory
Foston
West Lilling
Sutton-on-the-Forest
Sutton Park
Thornton-le-Clay
Crambe
Tollerton
Youlton
Kyle
Barton-le-Willows
Linton-on-Ouse
Flaxton
Harton
Howsham
18
A19
Strensall
Claxton
Bossall
Strensall Common
Newton-on-Ouse
Scrayingham
Nun Monkton
Beningbrough Hall (NT)
Shipton
Wiggington
Towthorpe
Sand Hutton
Buttercrambe
Beningbrough
B1363
Haxby
Earswick
Upper Helmsley
A64
Moor Monkton
Skelton
Stockton on the Forest
Stamford Bridge
A59
Overton
A1237
Huntington
Warthill
Roman Road
New Earswick
Gate Helmsley
Full Sutton
15
Nether Poppleton
Rawcliffe
Brockfield
A166
Stamford Bridge 1066
Marston Moor
Marston Moor 1644
Upper Poppleton
A19
A1036
Holtby
Low Catton
Hessay
Minster
High Catton
YORK
A59
Jorvik Viking Centre
Murton
Long Marston
Knapton
Nat Rly Museum
Osbaldwick
Dunnington
Rufforth
Acomb
Clifford's Tower
A1079
11
Wilberfoss
B1224
Hutton Wandesley
Kexby
Bilton
A1036
Heslington
Askham Bryan
A1237
York
Fulford
B1228
Newton upon Derwent
Angram
A64
Healaugh
Askham Richard
McArthurGlen
Elvington
Wighill
Bilbrough
10
Bishopthorpe
Copmanthorpe
Crockey Hill
Sutton upon Derwent
Catterton
Acaster Malbis
Naburn
Wheldrake
A64
Colton
Deighton
Storwood
Tadcaster
Escrick
Ross Moor
Acaster Selby
Thicket Priory
East Cottingwith
Kirkby Wharfe
Appleton Roebuck
Thorganby
Bolton Percy
Ouse
B1222
A162
Stillingfleet
A19
B1228
Ulleskelf
Wharfe
Ellerton
Towton
B1223
Ryther
Kelfield
Aughton
Skipwith
Foggathorpe
Cawood
Riccall
North Duffield
Saxton
Church Fenton
Barkston
Highfield
A163
Bubwith
Wistow
Little Fenton
Gunby
B1223
Biggin
Barlby
South Duffield
Ouse
B1228
Breighton
Sherburn in Elmet
B1222
Osgodby
Newthorpe
Thorpe Willoughby
Lund
Selby
Cliffe
Wressle
South Milford
Hambleton
Brind
Monk Fryston
8
Brayton
Hemingbrough
A63
12
Lumby
A63
Howden Sta.
Newsholme
3
A162
Hillam
Gateforth
7
Barlow
Long Drax
Barmby on the Marsh
Knedlington
Asselby
Burn
A1041
A1

STD Code 01904

YORK

1 **2** **3**

A19
Burton Stone Lane
York City F.C.
Grosvenor Rd.
York District Hospital
Wigginton Road
Haxby Road
Park Grove
City General Hospital
Huntington Road
Dodsworth Avenue
A1036 Malton Rd
Clifton
Grosvenor Terrace
Bootham Park Hospital
Clarence St.
Lowther Street
Penley's Grove St.
Heworth Green

A

N
Playing Fields
Bootham
Gillygate
Lord Mayor's Walk
John's St.
Monkgate
Foss Bank
Layerthorpe
East Parade
Glen Gardens
Fifth Avenue
Fourth Ave.
Bull Lane

River Ouse
Yorkshire Museum & St. Mary's Abbey (Ruins)
Art Gallery
York Minster
City Wall
Monk Bar
St. Maurice's Rd.
Aldwark
Archaeological Resource Centre
Hallfield Road
Theatre Royal
Museum Gardens
Museum St.
Petergate
Assembly Rooms
Goodramgate
St. Andrewgate
Shambles
The Stonebow
National Railway Museum
War Mem. Gdns.
P.O.
Mansion Ho.
Church St.
Fossgate
Leeman Road
Guildhall
Coney St.
Merchants Adventurers' Hall
River Foss
Foss Islands Road

B

Station Rd.
Rougier St.
North St.
Jorvik Viking Centre
Ousegate
Impressions Gallery
Red Tower
York Dungeon
Clifford St.
Walmgate
Queen St.
Micklegate
Skeldergate
Fairfax Ho.
Clifford's Tower
Castle Mus.
Piccadilly
Walmgate Bar
Micklegate Bar
City Wall
Law Courts
Crown Courts
Lawrence St.
A1079
Holgate Road
A59
Dalton Terr.
The Mount
Moss St.
Blossom St.
Nunnery Lane
Baile Hill
Bishopgate St.
Tower St.
Fishergate
City Wall
Paragon St.
Barbican Rd.
Heslington Road

C

A1036
Tadcaster Road
Albemarle Road
Scarcroft Hill
Scarcroft Road
Bishopthorpe Rd.
River Ouse
Barbican Centre (Leisure Cen. & Swimming Baths)
Cemetery Rd.
A19
Cemetery
Playing Fields
Southlands Road
Rowntree Park

YORK
100   0   400 yds
100   0   400m

BBC RADIO YORK 103.7 FM
MINSTER FM 104.7 FM

LOCAL RADIO

TOURIST INFORMATION ☎ 01904 554488
TIC TRAVEL OFFICE, 20 GEORGE HUDSON ST.,
YORK, YO1 6WR

HOSPITAL A & E ☎ 01904 631313
YORK DISTRICT HOSPITAL, WIGGINTON ROAD,
YORK, YO31 8HE

COUNCIL OFFICE ☎ 01904 613161
THE GUILDHALL,
YORK, YO1 9QN

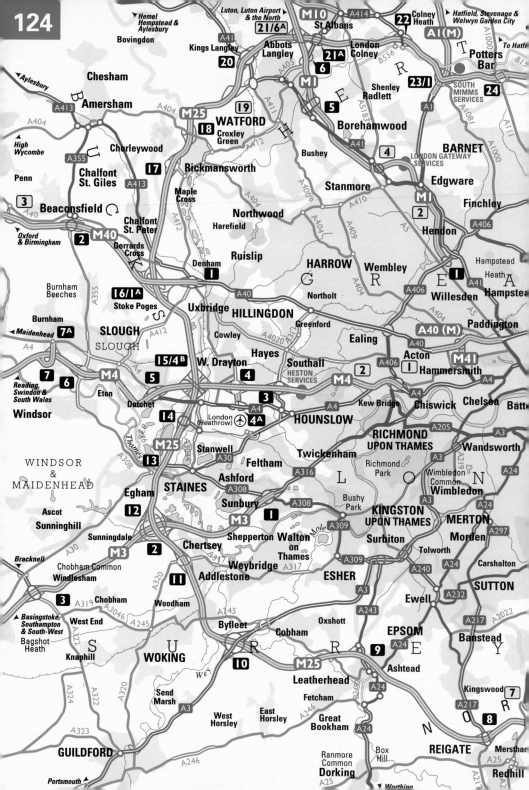

M25 · **M11** · **M20** · **M26** · **M23**

Ware & Hertford
Cuffley
B156
Cheshunt
M25
25
Waltham Cross
Waltham Abbey
Epping
Harlow, Stansted Airport & Cambridge
A414
A414

North Weald Bassett
6
27
26
Theydon Bois
Loughton
Epping Forest
Roding
A113
A128
Doddinghurst
Ingatestone
A12
Chelmsford, Ipswich & Harwich

Waltham Cross
Enfield Chase
Southgate
A10
Wood Green
Tottenham
Hornsey
Stoke Newington
Islington
A10
A501
City
Westminster
Camberwell
Brixton
A23
A202
Streatham
A23

Chingford
WALTHAM FOREST
Woodford
A406
Walthamstow
Leyton
Hackney
Bethnal Green
Poplar
Docklands
Greenwich
Lewisham
A205

Edmonton
Abridge
ESSEX
BILLERICAY
M25
BRENTWOOD
28
HAVERING
A12
Basildon & Southend
A127
Laindon
A128

CHIGWELL
Woodford
4
REDBRIDGE
A1400
A12
A11
A406
Wanstead
Ilford
BARKING
East Ham
Stratford
London City Airport
A102
A205
Woolwich
Thamesmead
A207

Romford
Hornchurch
Upminster
A127
29
B186
THURROCK
A13
Southend

Becontree
Dagenham
Rainham
A13
A1306
Thames
A1016
South Ockendon
30
THURROCK SERVICES
West Thurrock
A126
GRAYS
Chadwell St. Mary
Tilbury
A1089
31
A282
Purfleet

A2
A20
BEXLEY
Sidcup
A20
A205
Chislehurst
A21
Beckenham
BROMLEY
A222
A232
West Wickham
Orpington
Farnborough
A21

Dartford
A206
A226
Swanscombe
Northfleet
GRAVESEND
Rochester, Dover & Margate
A2
Istead Rise
Meopham
A227

1 A
1 B
Wilmington
A2018
Hextable
Swanley
M25
2 Darenth
3/1
South Darenth
Hartley
M20
New Ash Green
A2

CROYDON
A232
A2022
New Addington
Biggin Hill
A233
Warlingham
Coulsdon
A22
A23
Purley
Caterham
7
6
M25
8
Godstone
Oxted
M23
Crawley, E. Grinstead & Brighton

4
Eynsford
KENT
West Kingsdown
A20
A225
Otford
Kemsing
M26
A25
Sevenoaks
Borough Green
2 A
A20
M20
3
2
Maidstone & Folkestone
A227

5
Westerham
B2026
A25
A21
B2042
East Grinstead & Eastbourne
Tonbridge & Hastings

Scale: 0 — 2 — 4 miles / 0 — 2 — 4 — 6 kms

2 Full junction
2 Restricted junction

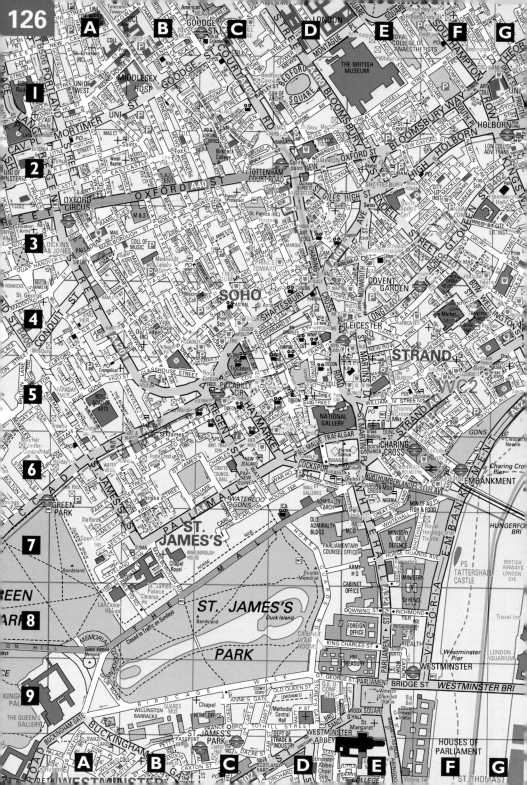

General Abbreviations

All.	Alley	Chyd.	Churchyard	Embk.	Embankment	Mkt.	Market
App.	Approach	Circ.	Circus	Est.	Estate	Mkts.	Markets
Arc.	Arcade	Clo.	Close	Gdn.	Garden	Ms.	Mews
Ave.	Avenue	Cor.	Corner	Gdns.	Gardens	Pas.	Passage
Bdy.	Broadway	Cres.	Crescent	Grd.	Ground	Pk.	Park
Bldgs.	Buildings	Ct.	Court	Gro.	Grove	Pl.	Place
Bri.	Bridge	Ct.	Courtyard	Ho.	House	Rd.	Road
Cen.	Centre,Central	E.	East	La.	Lane	Ri.	Rise

Sq.	Square
St.	Street,Saint
Sta.	Station
Ter.	Terrace
Twr.	Tower
Wf.	Wharf
Wk.	Walk
Yd.	Yard